LIVING
THE
BIBLICAL STORY

LIVING THE BIBLICAL STORY

EUGENE F. ROOP

ABINGDON
Nashville

LIVING THE BIBLICAL STORY

Library of Congress Cataloging in Publication Data

ROOP, EUGENE F   1942-
  Living the Biblical story.
  Bibliography: p.
  1.   Bible—Study—Text-books.   I.   Title.
BS605.2.R66   220'.07   79-13448

ISBN 0-687-22329-6

MANUFACTURED BY THE PARTHENON PRESS AT
NASHVILLE, TENNESSEE, UNITED STATES OF AMERICA

To my parents,
Lois E. and G. Frederic Roop,

who taught me the Bible
by living it as story

Contents

Preface

For the people of God, the Bible continues to be a living story. "Story" used in this way does not mean history or even narrative, although the Bible contains elements of both. Rather "story" refers to the literature which structures the life of a community. The Bible is such a structure for the life of the Christian community. Of course other literature is important, indeed indispensable, to Christians; however, the Jewish tradition is correct in understanding that all other literature is in a sense *commentary* on the Bible, the foundational story of the church. There is no substitute for constant, careful dialog with the Bible, our living story.

This book of case studies seeks to bring scholars and lay persons together in a vigorous study of the Bible. The cases have been used in quite diverse congregations and can be taught by a pastor or a lay person. They have been employed in church school education and for short term educational ventures such as conferences and retreats. These cases have been used in college and seminary classes. By involving the ordained and the unordained together in biblical study, the case method can contribute to the nurturing of faith and the strengthening of the common ministry of Christians.

These biblical cases have been developed with the financial and personal assistance of people too numerous to mention. The cases are indeed a product of the Christian community whose faith and ministry they seek to strengthen. Financial assistance came from the Association of Theological Schools through the Case Study Institute and from an ATS Curriculum Development Grant funded by the Lilly Foundation. This work would not have progressed had it not been for the support of the schools within whose context I worked, Earlham School of Religion and Bethany Theological Seminary. David Garman, Dena Pence Frantz, Elmer Martens, and Graydon Snyder made content contributions to specific cases. Tom Mullen of Earlham and Robert and Alice Evans of the Hartford Seminary Foundation helped polish the material. Several church congregations agreed to test the material and others had it "tested" on them when they invited me to lead a Bible study. The contribution made by my family can never be repaid. Delora, my wife, typed and retyped the manuscript and together with our children, Tanya and Frederic, gave up family time for the project.

Introduction:
The Bible and Case Study

Carlyle once wrote, "Experience is the best of schoolmasters, only the school fees are heavy." A case method approach to learning recognizes the importance of Carlyle's insight. When experience is our teacher, we learn quickly and we retain what we learn. A "case" starts with a moment of experience. It seeks to recapture that moment in written form in order that we might examine that experience and learn from it.

The case **The King and the Prophet** provides an example. It lifts up a moment in the experience of the kingdom of Judah. It is the moment in which Judah was threatened with immediate military defeat by a coalition army from the North. To that situation Isaiah proclaimed, "Behold, a young woman shall conceive and bear a son, and shall call his name Immanuel. . . . For before the child knows how to refuse the evil and choose the good, the land before whose two kings you are in dread will be deserted" (7:14, 16). Isaiah advised the king of Judah to do nothing, that deliverance would be forthcoming without any military action by Judah. Was Isaiah correct? Was it wise to risk letting Judah be conquered on the basis of a prophet's proclamation? Through a written case, we can experience this moment from the past; we can listen to Isaiah's proclamation and feel a bit of the agony of the king of Judah as he tried to decide what to do. Because experience is such an effective teacher, a case method approach to learning centers our attention on a moment of experience.

Nevertheless, the second part of Carlyle's proverb is as important as the first. We all remember well the lessons learned from the "school of hard knocks." However, sometimes the "knocks" are crippling or even fatal; the "school fees are heavy," sometimes too heavy. A child may learn to stay out of the street after being hit by a car, but the price is too high. A Christian can learn to face the issues surrounding death by personal experience, but often the lesson comes too late to be helpful. A case study approach enables us to learn from someone else's experience, but at a fraction of the cost.

A look at a case detailed in *Christian Theology: A Case Study Approach,* edited by Robert Evans and Thomas Parker, can provide an example. The experience reported is that of Marion Hathaway:

> Marion Hathaway's eyes filled with tears as she turned away from the vacant stare of her husband of fifty-one years. Two weeks before, George Hathaway had suffered the third stroke in as many days; he was completely paralyzed and could no longer speak. . . .
>
> Thorough testing by the hospital staff had given convincing evidence that the damage to George's nervous system was so extensive that there was no possibility for recovery of normal functions. . . . However, the heart condition had stabilized and the medical specialists now indicated that with intravenous feeding, oxygen, and later constant medical care in a nursing home, George could live for weeks, even months, or years.[1]

By involving ourselves in Marion's situation we may be able to learn from her experience. It is unlikely that precisely the same experience will happen to anyone of us. However, when a situation similar to Marion's touches our lives, we can carry some of the learning from her case into our own unique moment. This will enable us to respond from "experience."

A case method approach to learning seeks to take Carlyle's proverb seriously. One of the main purposes of this approach is to learn from experience at a fraction of the cost.

The Case Method and Religious Studies

A case study approach has long been used in churches, colleges, and seminaries to help Christians mature in their understanding of the faith. Such an approach has proven especially valuable in considering appropriate Christian responses to ethical situations. Issues like divorce, abortion, multi-national corporations, and homosexuality have been explored not hypothetically, but as real moments through the discussion of cases. A controversial case, "Consternation at Cactus Church," provides an example of education in ethical issues using the case method.[2] Tom Skelter, a new pastor, found the names of two of the congregation's retired members on the same mailbox. Ben Metzger and Bertha Kraemer were "pillars" of Cactus Church:

"No, we're not married, Pastor," said Ben. "We can't afford to be. It's just a common-sense living arrangement. Many of us out here have been forced into this kind of a situation. It's a simple matter of trying to stay alive. If Bertha and I got married it would be a financial disaster for both of us. One of us would lose much of our social security check. We'd forfeit our tax break—that's really substantial! You realize what I mean, Pastor? We just couldn't afford to eat and pay our medical bills. You know how hard it is just to exist today. . . ."

Someday laws may change so that the exact situation of Ben and Bertha will not arise, but the ethical issues in this case will remain alive. The problem of survival is old. The ethics of survival is a prominent theme in many of Charles Dickens' novels, e.g., *Oliver Twist.* One can see the same issues arising in periods when the church was persecuted. The case of Ben and Bertha illustrates again that these questions are here to stay. Christians can explore these continuing ethical concerns in their actual settings through the case method.

Case studies are increasingly being used to teach in areas other than ethics. Theology and history are as closely related to "real life" as are counseling and ethics. If we look again at the case involving Marion Hathaway, we find that it provides a wealth of options for exploring different areas of the Christian faith. It facilitates our coming to terms with death, both our own and the death of the ones we love most, which is an important area of counseling and pastoral care. The case also raises ethical questions regarding extra-ordinary activity to keep an unresponsive person alive and theological issues such as, What does it mean to talk about the providence of God in this situation? How can we understand God as the Creator and Sustainer of life when we are looking at a human vegetable?

Obviously it is valuable to start from actual life moments when we are exploring ethics and caring for the counseling dimensions of the church's life. Cases can also be the catalyst through which we discuss theology. By using cases for theology we keep our Christology and our anthropology directly connected to life as we experience it.

Biblical studies have probably employed the case method less than most other areas of religious studies. To be sure, there have been methods of Bible study which have emphasized the relationship between the Bible and our experience. One might mention the personal discovery approach of Lyman Coleman which is sometimes called "relational Bible study."[3] Important also is the "biblical simulation" approach of Donald Miller, Graydon Snyder, and Robert Neff.[4] Simulations are fun as well as instructive. Members of a group take different roles in a biblical situation and create an impromptu drama. The goal of a simulation is to experience the dynamics of a scene from the Bible. Case studies from the Bible share some of the goals of a simulation but use a discussion format seeking to stay closely connected with the history of a biblical event.

Since this is a book of biblical cases, it is important to define a "biblical case" as it is understood here. Although other kinds of cases might be called biblical, the cases in this book are especially concerned with lifting out real slices of life from the history of Israel and the New Testament church. For example, the case entitled **Sacred Space** concerns the struggle of the Jewish community over whether to rebuild the temple which was destroyed by the Babylonians while **Free at Last** centers on problems which arose in the Corinthian church when women and slaves in the Roman world began exercising the new freedom they had found in Christ.

There are many *real* moments in the Bible which we can experience and from which we can learn. Movies such as *The Ten Commandments, The Gospel According to St. Matthew,* and *Godspell* have attempted to dramatize some moments in history. The movie efforts vary in the extent to which they seek to be historically reliable. Some choose drama over history. My purpose in this book is to be as responsible with the history in the Old and New Testaments as possible. At the same time, case discussion can facilitate our experience of the realness of these moments.

Operative Assumptions

There are certain assumptions in the writing and use of biblical cases which need to be stated. The first assumption has already been mentioned. In this book the Bible is understood to be the result of lived moments in the community of faith. The narratives, poetry, and proclamation in the Bible issue forth from such moments. It is often difficult for us to internalize the fact that these were real people like ourselves. Case discussion seeks to help us do that by pushing us to relate moments in our lives with moments from ancient Israel and the New Testament church. We will look at the division among the people of Israel at the time of King Omri and also at divisions which rend our own communities. We will discuss the conflicts between "liberals" and "conservatives" in the New Testament church and similar conflicts within our own church.

Because biblical moments are from the past, more than a quick reading will be necessary to understand them. The biblical texts were written to an earlier audience. Since we are not the original audience, it is vital for us to "replay" the historical moment out of which the biblical passage came and to "rehear" the message which was intended for that earlier audience. We are then in a position to hear the word which the Bible has to speak to our moment.

In this regard what is required of us in understanding the Bible is not different from other written historical documents. We can misinterpret any document from the past if we are ignorant of the context within which it was written and the message it conveyed to that moment. The misinterpretation of the United States Declaration of Independence provides a familiar example. Untitled copies of that document were passed out to American citizens. The substantial number of people who did not recognize the declaration gave many different interpretations of the document. Frequently the declaration was interpreted as the subversive literature of a contemporary "left wing" group intent on "overthrowing" the United States government.

One certainly could not equate the Bible and the Declaration of Independence in terms of its wealth of meaning for the Christian. However, the process of understanding the two documents is similar. It is important that we understand the Bible in the context in which it was written. This enables us to hear better the message of the text to its day and to relate the document to our own day in a more careful way. To understand the Declaration of Independence in the context of the eighteenth century as a cry for freedom by a colonial people does not make the document any less relevant to our time. Rather it facilitates our awareness of its appropriate application in our own time. Hence, in our day the

Declaration of Independence may well serve as a warning against the problems created by overt and covert colonialism. As with the Declaration of Independence, the greatest impact of the letter of Paul to the church at Corinth is felt when we relive the moment out of which that letter arose.

There is a second assumption, closely related to the first, which needs to be mentioned. Biblical studies in the context of the church have a goal beyond that of replaying moments of history. Our task is not complete when we have understood the text as a moment from our past. We must go beyond analysis to understand the implications of the text for our own life. Krister Stendahl has stated that task as clearly as anyone.[5] He calls us to be able to function in two worlds, the world of the Bible and the contemporary world. We must be precise in our analysis of the Bible so we can hear the message it spoke to its own time. But we must also be students of our own day so that we can translate and speak the word to our time.

Alex Haley created an enormous interest in looking at one's past through the book *Roots* and the subsequent television program. Haley understood that the task was not simply to look at one's "roots" as a matter of curiosity, but to grasp how one's past affects one's present understanding of the world. As Stendahl insists, we must seek ways in which what we learn from our past can be translated into present action. This "translational" process is not automatic or easy. It takes a perceptive understanding of the present to make the translation appropriate and pertinent. Inappropriate translations of our past are frequent. For example, Alex Haley might have decided that his past called for vengeance against those families or that race that enslaved his ancestors. Such was not the effect. His translation of his slave past had a more positive program.

It is similar as we work with the Bible. The process of taking our understanding of the biblical message and translating it into a message understood in the present is called "hermeneutics." Biblical hermeneutics in the context of the church requires two things of any individual or group engaging in such activity. One must possess both a keen mind and a sensitive spirit. Perceptive analysis must be combined with an ability to be sensitive to the continuing presence of God in the world. Case studies seek to facilitate the process of understanding the Bible in its own time *and* translating the Bible for our time.

There is one final assumption which needs to be stated. The Bible arose in a community of faith. That community has preserved the Bible and it is appropriate that the Bible be studied and interpreted in a community setting. Unlike most of the literature with which we are acquainted, the Bible was not written by one person or at one time. It was written by persons of faith, some named, most unnamed, as they experienced God active in their midst. One can affirm that the Bible is not the product of individual human genius or even "superstars" of the faith, but the experience of the Spirit of God at work in and through the community. Hence the study of the Bible and the reinterpretation of it is a community task.

Until recently, the customary use of the Bible has been as an object of individual meditation and reflection. Two pictures come to our minds: a monk cloistered away from the frantic activities of the day intently at study and prayer, and a disciplined Christian involved in his or her early morning devotions reading a chapter from the Bible. Perhaps few of us fit these pictures, but for a long time these have been the dominant images of how a sincere Christian ought to use the Bible.

It is true, of course, that individual study of the Bible is important. However, as we increasingly come to understand the Bible as a product of the *community* of faith, it becomes questionable whether individual study and meditation on the Bible is the only productive image.

The case method calls us to an image of a community at study, working together to understand the Bible and translate its message. Certainly there have been such images of community in the past. The prayer and Bible study groups in churches and Sunday schools provide an example. In those settings a teacher would share what a particular text meant to him or her. Class members would then offer their perspective. Case method picks up on the group setting. However, it seeks to move the group from a collection of individuals sharing their own ideas to a community working in concert on a given text and the attendant issues.

The case method assumes that there is no individual, however perceptive, who can impart the whole answer to complex questions of life and faith. The case method trusts each one of the answers as it emerges from the group. Hence the role of the teacher is to facilitate and focus the discussion rather than to impart answers. The responsibility of a group member is to listen carefully to the contributions of others and to share his or her own ideas so that the discussion moves toward an understanding which the group as a whole can affirm. The goal is not that everyone be forced to conform to one conception of the biblical text and its message. The hope is rather that case-directed discussion will move individuals toward one another as they work with the biblical text and then outward, strengthened in their faith by their common ministry.

A community approach to Bible study is appropriate not only because we know that the Bible grew out of a faith community, but because we know how much we need community with one another. Gail Sheehy in *Passages* describes two aspects of each person, the "Seeker Self" and the "Merger Self."[6] The Seeker Self goes off on its own aiming to seek individuality. The Merger Self feels the urge to join with another or others to lose itself in a group. Gail Sheehy's central point is that we are essentially alone.[7] She says we must follow our Seeker Self, denying our Merger Self as a basis for relationship with others, because sooner or later we realize our aloneness, "our own absolute separateness."[8] While not denying the Seeker Self, the Christian faith says that it is appropriate to nurture the Merger Self, because ultimately we are not alone. In the Christian community, in the Body of Christ, we can savor our togetherness, our oneness.

A case study approach assumes that the Bible is most beneficially studied in community. This is appropriate because the Bible was preserved in and by a community. Such an approach allows expression of our "oneness in Christ Jesus" and recognizes that where "two or three are gathered in Christ's name," there is the Presence.

Goals of the Case Method

One of the primary goals of case study is listening, listening to one another, to the Bible, and to God. In using "cases" from the Bible as a focus of group discussion, it is essential that we be willing to listen to one another. None of us thinks of him or herself as a poor listener. However in a case discussion we will often find that we are not as careful listeners as we would like to be. At times we will feel as if others have not really heard what we have to say, and quite likely they will have the same experience of not being listened to.

One of the tasks of the leader is to help the listening process. The leader can help by calling a halt to further dialog until people have been clearly heard. This helps to keep the discussion focused. When the group is listening carefully to one another, each person's contribution will relate to that made by a previous speaker. By being a listener of listeners, the leader can guide the discussion and keep it related to issues raised in the case. This is quite a different role from the one in which the teacher is understood to provide information and solutions. The person who has what he or she considers the "correct" answers and feels compelled to deliver them as the solution usually does not make the best case teacher or leader. One teacher, after teaching a case, said, "It felt funny not to be telling the others what I think. Several times I wanted to jump in and give the 'answer.' But I must admit I liked the answer the group came to maybe even better than my own."

An important task of the leader is to listen, to help others listen, and to keep the discussion focused.

But our goal is not only to listen to one another, it is also to listen to the Bible. By studying together we have others to help us listen carefully to the text. Of course the group does not automatically insure that the text will be heard in a beneficial manner. Whole groups have heard the Bible calling for things which we now judge to be inappropriate. Communities have interpreted the Bible as supporting the enslavement of black Americans or the extermination of European Jews. Nevertheless, the group does help check the individual and serve to "rein us in" if our listening to the Bible goes too far astray.

Listening to God is the goal of our listening to one another and to the Bible. It is hoped that through this process we will be more sensitive to God's word for our day. We seek to listen carefully to God, because God first listened attentively to us. "And the people of Israel groaned under their bondage, and cried out for help, and their cry under bondage came to God. And God heard their groaning, and God remembered his covenant with Abraham, with Isaac, and with Jacob" (Exod. 2:23-24).

Let us turn from the listening goal to mention a couple of other goals. It is expected that through case study we will be stimulated to learn more about the Bible. It is often said that people in the church do not know the Bible, and it is common to find people feeling guilty or ashamed about their ignorance. A young couple stated the situation precisely:

> We realize that we ought to know more about the Bible. We have heard it preached; we have read the stories, but we can't get into it. We are left with only vague memories about the stories. How can we get into the Bible so that it engages us and is not just a series of meaningless stories and hard-to-pronounce names?

Of course there is no shortcut to making the Bible meaningful. Nevertheless part of the process is experiencing that the Bible is about real people whom we can understand and with whom we can identify. A case seeks to facilitate this by taking a slice from biblical life. We see people similar to us dealing with some of "our" problems. Omri had to solve the problem of seemingly irreconcilable division in the community. The Corinthian church agonized over the limits to freedom. The Jews struggled with the use and misuse of religious buildings.

As the Bible comes alive, we will be stimulated to work with it more, to pursue questions that arise out of our study together. Because we are discovering the Bible together, rather than being "told about it," the information may stay with us longer. We are learning by experience. As Carlyle said, that is the best of all schoolmasters.

There is yet another goal which might be mentioned. It is hoped that a case study approach to the Bible can facilitate the reintroduction of the Bible into the ethical issues of our day. It is everywhere evident that the Bible is being eased out of the discussion of ethical problems. James Smart in his book, *The Strange Silence of the Bible in the Church*, points out that the "newness" of our time has caused many people to see the Bible as irrelevant.[9] We are so convinced of the distance between our time and life in ancient Israel and the New Testament church that we ignore the Bible as we grapple with living. A college student stated this feeling dramatically: "The Bible is 'off the wall' on most issues and silent on the rest."

It is not the time gap alone that is responsible for the problem. The Bible has been misused. A panel discussion in a local church on the role of women featured some persons quoting "scripture" to support a subordinant or secondary role for women while other panel members referred only to texts which supported the equality of women. In a discussion about civil disobedience a similar thing happened. The group that opposed "law breaking" stood resolutely on a "Jesus quotation": "Render unto Caesar the things that are

Caesar's." The group that felt civil disobedience was appropriate used another "Jesus quotation": "No one can serve two masters." The Bible soon loses its value when it is used as a source book of "proof texts."

Hence our distance from the biblical setting and the manipulation of the Scriptures for our own ends are two reasons why the Bible has dropped out of the dialog over contemporary issues. Yet there remains the conviction that if we are to call ourselves Christians, the Bible must be taken seriously. The Bible must be allowed to speak on contemporary issues as difficult and hazardous as that may be. To be sure it is a new time. The Bible knows nothing about the DNA molecule. Nevertheless, there are issues that arise from the experimentation with DNA with which the Bible does struggle. For example, God gave to David the freedom to shape Israel's life and institutions. The narrative of Israel's slide into the Babylonian Exile is the story of the mismanagement of that responsibility. Instead of using their position to enhance life, the powerful people destroyed life in ancient Israel by political, economic, and religious mismanagement. Their whole life came to be oriented away from the one who brought them up out of Egypt. We too have a mandate to shape our life. If we mismanage our life together, disaster will result for us. How can we manage our scientific advances in such a way that life is enhanced and we are faithful to the Author of DNA?

It is one goal of the case method to reintroduce the Bible into the discussion of ethical questions in a responsible way. Each case will encourage us to consider the dynamics of a moment in biblical history, then to move from that to our moments. It is certainly possible to misrepresent the Bible in this process. However hazardous it may be, one goal of this approach is to end the disquieting silence of the Bible in the church and responsibly relate the Bible to issues which press us for a Christian response.

A Distinction

Many of us are familiar with cases used in other fields of study. Business, medicine, and law are three areas which have used the case method in their education. In medicine, "cases" are used to teach students diagnostic skills. In business schools cases are used to enable students to learn to confront and respond creatively to problems that arise in business management. Persons preparing for the legal profession assimilate legal principles and precedents by discussing actual cases.

Although biblical cases have many things in common with these other approaches, there is at least one element that is distinctive. Although there may be a "decision focus" in a biblical case, if we turn to the appropriate biblical text, we find out not only what decision was made, but often how that decision was evaluated. For example, **Dealing with a Defeat** lifts out a moment when Israel was deciding whether or not to become a monarchy. It is not hard to find out that Israel did decide to crown a king. Furthermore, a bit more reading will give us the information about how the writers of I and II Kings evaluated Israel's monarchs. But if the Bible continues to be a meaningful story for Christians what then is there for us to discuss today?

Even though a biblical case may center on a decision-making moment, the discussion of the case can move beyond that point. The group may focus on the dynamics leading up to the decision. In the case **Dealing with a Defeat** the discussion will likely deal less with whether or not Israel should select a monarch and more with the benefits and liabilities of the people of God institutionalizing their system of leadership. **The Conscience and the Community** centers on the matter of what the Corinthian community should do with food that had been blessed by a *pagan* priest. In I Corinthians we find Paul's answer to that problem. Hence the discussion may go beyond that decision and focus on understanding "conscience" and the ways in which the conscience can function creatively or destructively in the community. Paul apparently did not use conscience to refer to the parental "no" which has been so vividly described by psychology. That element in the human experience which Paul labeled "conscience" was a freeing and not a restrictive element.

An important distinction between biblical cases and those in areas such as business, medicine, and law arises because of the character of the Bible for Christians. Although the decision-making moments of biblical cases are reported and evaluated in an ancient document, Christians still experience this story as being true in their own life and faith today. The issues surrounding those particular moments are very much related to our time.

Case Teaching

Certainly for those coming to the case method for the first time it is the teaching of cases that raises anxiety. It is different from more traditional teaching responsibilities. This is due in part to the fact that the case method attempts intentionally to blur the distinction between teachers and learners because all participants in a case discussion are learners and teachers.

Having said that, there still remains a role for a discussion leader or "teacher." Stated simply, the teacher's role is to select a goal for the discussion of the case and to guide the discussion toward that goal. This single statement needs to be expanded briefly.

1. It is the task of the teacher to study the material and to have selected a goal toward which he or she wants the discussion to go. It is also important to have a plan for guiding the flow of the discussion. This can consist of an outline which projects the movement of the discussion. A discussion period with no direction is not too likely to be productive.

2. During the discussion, the teacher can assist the discussants in keeping their comments directed and related. It is also important to notice how people are acting in the

discussion and to find ways to facilitate the entrance of those who are more reticent. The case method assumes that each individual brings important ideas or information to contribute to the case discussion.

3. It is important that the teacher remain flexible regarding the goal and direction of the discussion. It may become appropriate in the process of the discussion for the direction which the teacher had envisioned to be changed. One of the difficult tasks for many teachers is to maintain a balance between a clear goal and a spontaneous flow of ideas. Many teachers have found it helpful to guide the discussion in the originally selected direction until there are indications of a broad consensus among the participants to move it in a new direction.

There is no single way to teach any given case. A great deal depends on the style of the teacher. Much also depends on the goal chosen for the discussion. And of course the setting and "personality" of the group will affect the way a case is taught. These three factors: teachers, goal, and class setting, will determine what the group as a whole is asked to do. In some situations it may be appropriate for the books to be handed out in class, having the members read only the case itself and perhaps the introduction to a particular case. In other situations all the participants may read the material in the "Communiqué to Learners and Teachers" and some of the additional reading suggested in "Resources to Read" ahead of time.

The "Directions for Discussion" which accompany each case are to be understood within the context of what was said immediately above: there is no single way to teach any given case. The suggestions in "Directions for Discussion" are geared toward educational work in a local congregation. They assume the discussion will focus on current issues which arise out of a case. This will not fit the goal of every group who might use these cases. For example, a college or seminary class in biblical studies may wish to focus more on the historical and analytical issues which are woven into the cases. **One Nation, Two Gods** can initiate a study comparing the religion of Yahweh and the religion of Baal. Or the discussion can be turned to focus on the way current historians differ in their understanding of this particular period of Israel's history.[10] I cannot stress too much that the teacher should not feel bound by the suggestions I have made for teaching each case, but should plan a discussion which fits his or her own style, goals, and class.

Perhaps there is no more important advice to be given to those using the case method for the first time than—Relax! The role of case teacher may be different from other teaching roles that you have experienced. Nevertheless the successful outcome of the discussion does not rest solely on the leader's shoulders. In a case discussion everyone is a teacher and all are learners.

Notes

1. Robert A. Evans and Thomas D. Parker, eds., *Christian Theology: A Case Study Approach* (New York: Harper and Row, 1976), p. 80.

2. "Consternation at Cactus Church" (Louisville, Ky.: The Case Study Institute, 1975).

3. Lyman Coleman, *Kaleidoscope* (Newton, Pa.: The Halfway House, 1969), is one example from the series of books he has published.

4. See their books *Using Biblical Simulations,* Vols. I and II (Valley Forge, Pa.: Judson Press, 1973).

5. Krister Stendahl, "Biblical Theology, Contemporary" in *The Interpreter's Dictionary of the Bible,* Vol. A–D (Nashville: Abingdon, 1962), pp. 418-31, especially p. 430.

6. Gail Sheehy, *Passages* (New York: Bantam Books, 1976), pp. 50-52.

7. *Ibid.* See among others pp. 416, 436, and 488.

8. *Ibid.,* p. 436.

9. James Smart, *The Strange Silence of the Bible in the Church* (Philadelphia: Westminster Press, 1970).

10. An example of such a lesson plan can be found in my "Teaching Note for One Nation, Two Gods." This lesson plan may be obtained from Intercollegiate Case Clearing House, Soldiers Field, Boston, Massachusetts 02163.

Part I
Shaping the Community

There are some issues with which every group must wrestle. The resolution of these matters deeply affects the shape and character of a group. One such concern is the matter of leadership. No group can avoid decisions about how leaders are to be selected and the role which leaders are to assume. The mission or purpose of the group is yet another community shaping issue. The cases in this first section, Part I, tend to concentrate on such community *shaping* concerns. Part II, Living as a People, deals with problems that arise as the people of God *live* out their life together.

There is no pretense that this casebook is exhaustive of all the possible issues which affect the shape or arise out of the life of the community. Nor can one say that there is an absolute distinction between those issues which shape the character of a community and those which emerge in the course of the community's life. What is expected is that these cases will facilitate our study of the Bible in concert with addressing important concerns which affect our Christian life together.

The four cases in Part I are taken from both the Old and the New Testament. The first case, **Dealing with a Defeat,** comes from a moment early in Israel's history. Leadership, and in particular the institutionalization of leadership, is a prime focus in this case. **Sacred Space** comes from the history of the Jewish people after their return from the Babylonian Exile. They had to struggle with the assets and liability of buildings set aside for worship. **Free at Last** is a case taken from the New Testament, specifically from the life of the Corinthian community. This new church struggled to develop a structure which would allow persons to express their new freedom in Christ while preserving an essential orderedness in the community. **The Role of Moses** was placed in Part I because it is a different approach to biblical case study. Although it involves a moment in the history of Israel, the Exodus, it does not really work with the moment of history in the way the previous cases do. Rather this case concentrates on the narrative describing the event. The Exodus narrative presents two portraits of the role of Moses and in so doing points us toward the question of the mission for the people of God.

1.

Dealing with a Defeat

Introduction

Periodically, athletic teams change managers or coaches. Only rarely is the coach fired when the team is winning. Almost predictably the manager of a losing team will soon be out of a job. There are many reasons why the manager of a losing team may be dismissed. It may be that someone has to take the blame and the coach is the easiest person to replace. The management of a team may know that a new coach will not make much difference, but out of frustration they have to do something. So they fire the coach.

However, there is another reason for changing managers. It may be clear from the way a team is organized and managed that the inevitable result will be defeat. Hence, it is hoped that a different organization using the same resources might have a different result. The players and their skills may not change, but if they are pulled together in a slightly different way, it might be enough to turn defeat into victory.

A similar situation faced Israel near the end of the eleventh century B.C. As the case material will relate, Israel had been defeated in a battle with the Philistines. What could Israel do to change defeat into victory the next time out? Obviously they could not change the players. They may have wished to trade a few of their people for some really strong Egyptians, but that was not a possibility. One possibility was to change the organization. For Israel that meant more than just firing the coach. It would mean a complete restructuring of their way of working together. Perhaps they could survive if they had a king. For Israel the question was much more severe than whether the team finished first in its division. It was a matter of whether or not Israel could survive as a people, as the people of God.

The Case Study

The Philistines fought and Israel was defeated. Everyone fled to their own home because the slaughter was enormous. Thirty thousand Israelite soldiers fell and the ark of God was captured. (I Sam. 4:10-11a)

Never had such a thing happened to the confederation of tribes called Israel. The people experienced the defeat as a disaster of monumental proportions. According to the narrative, among those lost in the battle was Phinehas, the son of Eli, the priest in Shiloh.

Now his [Eli's] daughter-in-law, the wife of Phinehas, was pregnant, about to give birth. When she heard the news about the capture of the ark of God . . . she collapsed and gave birth. . . . And the women attending her said, "Do not be afraid for you have had a son." But she did not answer or pay attention. She named her son, "No glory" [Ichabod]. . . . She said, "The glory has departed from Israel because the ark of God has been captured." (I Sam. 4:19-22)

A question of survival arose out of this despair. Could Israel continue to exist as a loose confederation of groups of people?

The Confederation

In the eleventh century B.C., it was hardly possible to speak of Israel as a nation. There were settlements near one another, and the people in these settlements were related to one another and shared the same faith. In times of danger they would band together under the leadership of a "Spirit-directed" leader called a "judge." Gideon was such a person:

All the Midianites . . . assembled and crossed over and camped in the Jezreel Valley. The Spirit of Yahweh took control of Gideon and he blew the trumpet. The clan of Abiezer assembled to follow him. And he sent messengers throughout Manasseh and they too assembled to follow him. Furthermore, he sent messengers to Asher, Zebulun, and Naphtali; they came to join them. (Judges 6:33-35)

This system of defense had been sufficient to deal with all threats until the Philistine challenge.

Suddenly there was a critical change. Previously the external threats had been limited both in time and place. Israel's enemies attacked in one place and each crisis was soon over. However, from the Philistines Israel faced widespread and constant pressure. Finally the makeshift, "ad hoc" army was not able to cope, the ark was captured. Israel had lost the battle.

Options

One possibility was a new type of leadership, leadership that had more power to act, a life-time judge.

The day before Saul's coming, Yahweh had revealed this to Samuel: "Tomorrow, about this time, I will send to you a man from the land of Benjamin. You shall anoint him to rule over Israel and he will save my people from the hand of the Philistines for I have seen the dilemma of my people and their cry has come to me." (I Sam. 9:15-16)

33

Saul, as an anointed ruler, would provide continuity and stability in leadership. This might enable Israel to deal with the constant threat to its existence in a way that was not possible with short periods of Spirit-directed leadership.

Nevertheless, there were problems for Israel in having a king. Some groups strenuously objected to kingship. Jotham's fable (Judges 9:7-15) represents one such protest. In this political allegory, the trees of the forest decided to anoint one of their number to rule over them. The crown was offered to all the able trees: the olive, the fig, even the grapevine. But none of these would accept the crown. They considered their present tasks far more worthwhile than being king. Finally the crown was offered to a fruitless nuisance, the bramble. The bramble not only accepted the crown, but demanded that all the other trees come under its protection and authority. This biting fable implied that a king is worthless and absurd. There would be nothing gained by a monarchy for Israel.

A theological objection to kingship was set forth in a speech which Samuel made to the people:

Thus says Yahweh, the God of Israel, "I alone brought you up out of the land of Egypt and I rescued you from the hand of the Egyptians and from the hand of all the kingdoms that were oppressing you. But today, you reject your God who saved you from all calamities and difficulties and you have said, "Set a king over us. . . ." (I Sam. 10:17-19a)

Giving up ad hoc, Spirit-called leadership for the continuity and stability of a monarch would be a theological disaster according to the perspective represented by Samuel in this speech. It would mean rejecting God's immediate leadership and setting a king between God and the people.

Another speech anticipates still another problem with a king:

This will be the custom of the king who rules over you: He will take your sons and make soldiers of them: charioteers, cavalrymen, and men running before his chariots, . . . and some to plow his field and to reap his harvest and to make his military hardware. . . . He will take your best field, vineyards, and olive orchards and give them to his servants. He will take a tenth of your grain and your grapes to give to his officers and servants. . . . He will take a tenth of your flocks and you will be to him like slaves. (I Sam. 8:11-17)

A ruler who would be strong enough to deal with the Philistine threat would be strong enough to treat people like servants. Such a person could practically make them slaves!

A strong central government would create major problems, both theological and social. Yet a weak government seemed unable to handle the Philistine challenge that threatened Israel's very existence.

Communiqué to Teachers and Learners

Directions for Discussion

Many people discussing this case may know that Israel decided on a monarchy. It is also well known that this was a mixed blessing. It is the reason for and against having a monarch that will stimulate discussion. There are different ways to instigate that dialog. The following is just one possibility.

A. Understanding the options. It is usually helpful at the start to get before the class the value and liability of a monarchy and the "judge," or Spirit-directed style of leadership. The class might begin by compiling a list of "pros and cons" for each style. The group might also do a short role play. A small group could take the roles of the "elders of Israel" debating the matter with some pleading for the monarchy and others arguing for the "judge" system. It is important to get out the reasons which are explicit in the case, but it is also desirable to go beyond that to "pros and cons" which are often implicit in the case. It is right at the juncture between what is explicit and what is not explicit that people may begin to relate the biblical moment to our time.

A list of the values of each leadership mode might include the following:

Monarchy	Judge
a. institutional continuity	a. spontaneity
b. stability	b. chosen for a specific moment
c. dependability	c. clearly dependent on God

Hopefully the group will have others they will add to this very partial list. The liabilities of each leadership form are the reverse side of the values, but the group may want to list these along with or instead of the values.

B. Evaluating the decision. In light of the list of pros and cons for each option, how do you respond to Israel's decision to go ahead with the monarchy? Those who think that Israel should not have crowned a king need to face Israel's problem with the Philistines. According to the case, the "judge" system had not been effective against the Philistine threat, and the destruction of Israel as a people seemed probable. Is any action to be taken in response to that threat? Those class members who think that kingship was the appropriate way for Israel to go need to face the problems that go along with that decision. What is to be done about the seemingly inevitable abuse of power that comes with a strong centralized government?

Of course our first inclination is to suggest an alternative leadership form, especially a democracy, but we remember that democracy was not an option at that time.

C. Leadership alternatives in our time. The next step might be to consider the various alternatives in our time. Does democracy resolve all the problems which were inherent in the alternative of "judge" or monarch? What are the liabilities of a democracy? Some people have argued that the United States came very close to a dictatorship in the thirties and forties because a democracy was not able to handle the enormous problems of economic depression and world war, a crisis not unlike that which Israel faced.

Many people, when they are thinking of different forms of leadership, look first at our civil government. Certainly it is important that one look there, but don't the same questions of leadership arise in other groupings? Look at the church either on the congregational or denominational level. What are the advantages of centralizing the leadership of the congregation in a strong pastor? What are the disadvantages? Look also at the possibilities for decentralizing the leadership of the church. We may be able to learn something from the "judge" system of ancient Israel. That would mean a congregation would have a strong, centralized leadership only to meet an emergency for a short period of time. Are there ways in which this "ad hoc," spontaneous leadership mode is or could be implemented in a congregation?

Nor is the church the only place where questions of leadership arise. Families might look at the system of leadership within the home. How would you characterize your home? In some families the leadership is firmly institutionalized. It may be centralized in one person or divided between two persons, but it is very well established. Such a situation provides steady, stable leadership for the family. In other families leadership is much more spontaneous. Even relatively young children can find themselves leading the family at important moments. Do you know families or can you recall times in your own family when decisions have been made or activities directed not by the "institutionally authorized" leader, usually a parent, but spontaneously and creatively by other family members? Many families remember these as some of their most exciting moments. How much spontaneity in leadership is beneficial to a family? When is such a leadership style detrimental?

D. Summary. One way to work with this case is as follows:

1. What are the values and liabilities of a monarchy and of a "judge" system for Israel?
2. Do you agree with Israel's decision to have a king?
3. In our own lives where do we find the same two conflicting systems of leadership—continuity and ad hoc? What are some of the assets and liabilities of each system?

Concerns to Consider

Among the issues which arise in this case, two stand out. One is the governance issue. Leadership centralized in a strong person presents different possibilities and problems than short-term leadership selected "ad hoc," that is, for a specific task. A second issue focuses on the security and vulnerability of the people of God. There are times when Christians are called to risk their very existence in response to God. Are there times when God calls Christians to take steps to insure their continued existence as a people?

A. For now or for all seasons. During the period of loose confederation, Israel selected leaders to meet specific crises. They chose leaders "for now." When the crisis, the "now," was over, the leader resumed his or her previous life. A church congregation will often designate a leader "for now." This may happen when a disaster strikes a community. The disaster might be a flood, hurricane, or tornado. The congregation organizes to provide relief to the victims. The first step may be to designate a person as a "disaster relief coordinator." The task of such a person is to assess the needs of the situation and assist the church to respond to those needs. When the task is done, the role of "disaster relief coordinator" will likely disappear or at least the person so designated will cease to function in that capacity. Another example of an ad hoc or "for now" leader is the "chairperson of the building committee." Such a person is chosen because of special qualifications to do that job at that moment. When the building is completed there is no longer a "chairperson of the building committee."

"For now" leadership is task oriented. There is a job to do. It is of limited scope and limited time. A person is chosen to do the job who is especially gifted in that area. We recognize that such gifts come from God and such a person is called by God to provide leadership "for now."

Sometimes we find such ad hoc leadership does not work. There was a congregation that struggled with how to be sure that persons in the hospital received regular visitation. It was too much for the pastor alone. The first attempt to solve the problem was on an "ad hoc" basis: "Announce it on Sunday morning and through the newsletter and someone will go and visit." This did not work. Some people were visited and some were not. So they decided to designate a member as the "minister of visitation." That would provide a continuity and consistency in meeting the task. This was similar to the response Israel made as the people moved toward replacing a "judge" with a "king."

Permanent, or "for all season," leadership has one major advantage over ad hoc or "for now" leadership. That is continuity. The calling will always get done because there is always a "minister of visitation." Such a person receives all calls from the hospital or the patient's family and is prepared to respond constantly. The congregation never has to worry about who will go and visit. No one will feel slighted because he or she was not visited. The congregation does not have to depend on a whim of the moment to move someone to get into a car and go to visit at the hospital.

However, there are some problems with such permanent or "for all seasons" leadership. Continuing with the congregation's attempts to get its people visited in the hospital, the congregation thought of a woman whom all agreed was right for the job. She had the ability to really meet and minister to the ill. The trouble was that she felt she did not have the time to take the job on a long-term basis. Hence, the congregation had to ask *first* who was available and then make the appointment. They appointed another person and the job was done, but not nearly as well as it would have been done by an especially gifted person. At times the man who was eventually appointed as "minister of visitation" got into his car and went to the hospital out of duty and not out of real willingness. At first he started out as "minister of visitation" out of desire, but when the need arose right in the middle of a family outing or a good night's sleep, it became duty and not the Spirit that got him into the car and to the hospital. About a year later, the congregation looked at the problem again. The appointee had quit. In the discussion one comment went as follows: "When we have an unskilled person visiting out of duty rather than desire, it might be better to have no 'minister of visitation.' Maybe we ought to forget a permanent office and depend on the Spirit to move someone to do the calling!" How do we decide which is preferred, Spirit-directed leadership "for the moment" or permanent leadership "for all seasons"?

B. Endanger or insure. Another issue involves the question of risk. If Israel were to remain with the "Spirit-directed," "judge" style of leadership, the risk was enormous. The people might not survive as an identifiable group, but be swallowed up in a Philistine empire. Certainly that is one of the main problems with spontaneous leadership. It may be weak when it needs to be strong. Spontaneous leadership may be more exciting and creative, and even, as in the case of Israel, more immediately related to God's leadership, but should a group risk its future by depending on leadership to arise when the occasion demands?

The push for institutional survival is a common phenomenon. Institutions generally take the steps necessary to insure their survival. News accounts document this in private higher education. During the sixties when survival was less of an issue, a number of colleges adopted an organizational style that was decentralized, broadly participatory. Now, however, some of these institutions are faced with the question of survival. Many have decided that they can no longer afford the luxury of such spontaneity and freedom in organization. They have to tighten up the organization. In some cases this means bringing in a strong president who can cut costs, find students, and raise money. These steps it is hoped will insure their survival.

The position of Samuel, as reflected in the biblical excerpts, calls on the institution to risk destruction by maintaining a more spontaneous leadership style. This is consistent with the words in Matthew 10:39. "The one who tries to gain life will lose it, but whoever loses their life for my sake will gain it." This would seem to indicate that the drive to survive is wrongheaded. Is it wrong to take steps to survive as Israel did by changing to centralized government, as many private colleges and universities are doing? To the contrary, some texts referred to in the case indicate that God endorsed Israel's move to survive by anointing Israel's king.

There is another way some choose to resolve the conflict between the call to risk and the need to survive: to maintain the "judge" system in the face of the Philistine threat would be the ideal. That is what Israel ought to have done, but practical circumstances forced the people to go a different way. Taking a less than ideal option in the interest of survival is sometimes necessary, although never perfect. We need an ideal to remind us of where we are heading, but in the present world we cannot actualize the ideal. It is all right for institutions and individuals to take necessary steps to survive as long as they don't lose sight of the ideal. Is this an adequate way to handle the problem? Does the Bible understand this *willingness* to risk death on the part of institutions and individuals as an unrealizable ideal or as a way to genuine survival?

Resources to Read

Judges 8:22–9:57; I Samuel 8–11

Israel's first experience with a monarchy was a fiasco. The people could not get Gideon to accept the post and Abimelech gave them nothing but trouble. The text shows the ambivalence that they felt toward trying again. Was Saul a savior sent by God or a frustrated demand for change by an unfaithful people?

Rendtorff, Rolf. *God's History: A Way Through the Old Testament.* G. C. Winsor, tr. Philadelphia: Westminster Press, 1969. Pp. 27-35.

The primary problem with the organization was that there was no full-time leader. Was a king or a "judge" better to lead the people against an enemy? The story of the installation of Saul reflects the domestic quarrel which arose over this question. This quarrel was never quite silenced in later generations.

Mowinckel, Sigmund. *He That Cometh.* G. W. Anderson, tr. Nashville: Abingdon Press, 1954. Pp. 21-95.

Israel had plenty of neighbors who had kings and Mowinckel discusses just about all of them! What did Israel copy from them? Was there anything different in Israel's understanding of a king? Mowinckel finds the distinctiveness in the absolute subordination of the king to God and the primary task of the king, namely to be God's instrument for justice and blessing.

Herrmann, Siegfried. *A History of Israel in Old Testament Times.* J. Bowden, tr. Philadelphia: Fortress Press, 1975. Pp. 131-41.

Saul was not a success as a king. He was not given much power. He had no court, no administration. He came to an office that the people could not agree on. They had never done it that way before. He was tried beyond his abilities.

2.
Sacred Space

Introduction

The Oakland Mills Uniting Church in Columbia, Maryland, has no building of its own. The congregation assembles at The Meeting House, a building which houses several different Christian and Jewish groups. There are few territorially identified spaces except for offices. Furthermore, there are no permanent religious symbols displayed and no permanent furniture in the places where the various groups worship.

The Oakland Mills Uniting Church was started as a new congregation at a time when the city itself was just beginning. This congregation, along with the others who share The Meeting House, has tried to organize its life without a clearly identifiable sanctuary, or sacred space, as we have come to know it in American Christianity. So far, the Oakland Mills Uniting Church is going quite well. They have had their struggles. One of them has been over the question of "sacred space." On the one hand, they have freedom to move in new directions of mission unencumbered by expensive, single-purpose facilities. On the other, the inter-faith facility has not provided the congregation with a space which they can call their own, a territory with their name on it which could function as a point of unity for the group. Oakland Mills Uniting Church is seeking other ways to symbolize its unity and to handle the need for identifiable sacred space.

Following years of exile in Babylon, Israel was permitted by Cyrus, the Persian monarch, to gather itself together and to reformulate its religious structures in Palestine. Permission to build a new temple was the cornerstone in this program. While this is not the same situation as the Oakland Mills Uniting Church, some of the problems are similar.

Would it be beneficial for the people to build a temple? They had had a temple in the past. This temple, built while Solomon was king, had provided Israel with an identifiable place to go to worship Yahweh. It was a source of strength and unity for the people. However, Israel's deep attachment to the temple also caused problems. The people thought that through worship at the temple their relationship to God was insured and their responsibility to God taken care of. Jeremiah states that Israel's inappropriate attachment to this sacred space was the reason God allowed the destruction of the temple by Babylon.

It was a new moment. Israel had to address the question of sacred space. Should they build a temple?

The Case Study

Is this a time for you to live in your paneled houses, while this House lies in ruins? So now, Yahweh of Hosts says this: "Reflect carefully how things have gone for you. You have sown much but harvested little; you eat but never have enough. . . . Why? declares Yahweh of Hosts. Because while my House lies in ruins you are busy with your own, each one of you." (Hag. 1:4-9)

The temple of Israel's God lay in ruins. Cyrus had given the people permission to rebuild the temple more than a decade earlier. Little had been done. Haggai unleashed a prophetic barrage denouncing the apathy of the people concerning their temple. The temple was the place where the glory of God was experienced in the midst of Israel. It was the spot where the encounter between Yahweh and God's people happened. It was sacred space. Such neglect of the religious dimension of life had serious consequences. It affected the basic quality of life. The people must have a place in which to worship. Not just any place, but the place where God had designated.

Zechariah agreed with Haggai. The people must support the governor's efforts to rebuild the temple: "Yahweh, then, says this. 'I turn again in compassion to Jerusalem; my Temple shall be rebuilt there' " (Zech. 1:16). The temple would be a symbol of renewal and unity to people scattered by the Exile.

But not everyone agreed. Isaiah of the Restoration condemned the rebuilding of the temple. Isaiah also spoke in Yahweh's name:

> Heaven is my throne, and the earth is my footstool.
> Is this a house you build for me?
> Is this a place where I am to rest? (Isa. 66:1)

Isaiah saw no need for the people to build a place set apart for worship, a sacred space. Yahweh needed no dwelling place:

> For thus says the high and lofty One
> who inhabits eternity,
> whose name is Holy:
> "I dwell in the high holy place,
> and also with the lowly and humble spirit, . . ." (Isa. 57:15)

A temple built by human hands could not enhance the religious character of the people. Sacred space was of little value. A new temple would not advance the central mission which was to bring new life to an oppressed people.

> He sent me to bring good news to the poor,
> to bind up broken individuals,
> to proclaim release to the captives;

to free those in prison;
to announce the year of Yahweh's favor,
and the day of our God's vengeance. (Isa. 61:1*b*-2)

Words from Israel's History

Tradition held that the first Israelite temple at Jerusalem was built by Solomon at God's direction.

Now I [Solomon] intend to build a temple for the name of Yahweh, my God, in response to the speech of Yahweh to David, my father: "Your son whom I will place on your throne to succeed you shall be the one to build a temple for my name." (I Kings 5:5)

After the temple had been destroyed by the Babylonians, Ezekiel prophesized that the restoration would include a new temple (see Ezek. 40). The temple was central to the faith. The people needed a space where they could go with the expectation that there they would meet Yahweh, their God.

On the other hand, Isaiah of the Restoration also had history behind his announcement that Yahweh did not want a temple. Tradition had preserved the word of God announced by the prophet Nathan when David had first desired to build a temple:

Are you going to build a temple for me to dwell in? I have never dwelt in a temple from the day in which I brought Israel up out of Egypt until this day. Rather I have always moved about in a tent and similar dwellings. (II Sam. 7:6)

A new temple was not central in Jeremiah's portrayal of the restoration either. The previous temple caused trouble because of the people's attachment to it (see Jer. 7). According to Jeremiah, Israel would be restored to the land, but a new covenant "written on the heart" would be central to the restored life, rather than a renewal of a sacred space.

47

Communiqué to Teachers and Learners

Directions for Discussion

In this case the focus is on a moment late in Israel's biblical history. As mentioned in the introduction, this was a time when the old structures of the Israelite religion had been destroyed and the new structures were just beginning to emerge. Should a new temple be one of those structures? By starting with this question facing Israel, a group can be led to explore the benefits and problems that accompany sanctuaries and church buildings for current religious communities.

A. Examining both sides. One avenue of entry into the discussion is to look at the reasons for and against building a new temple. Such a point of departure helps to plant the particulars of the case firmly in the minds of the group. Many church groups who discuss this issue are predisposed in favor of building the temple. If the discussion leader expects that to be the case, it sometimes promotes interest to begin with the other side, "What are the reasons why the Jews should *not* rebuild the temple?" Among the reasons that are mentioned, the following frequently appear in one form or another:

1. A temple is a basic misunderstanding of how God relates to Israel.
   a. Yahweh cannot be bound to one place (II Sam. 7).
   b. The dwelling place of God is "above and among the people" (Isa. 57).
2. Building and maintaining a temple takes energy away from Israel's important mission (Isa. 61).
3. Prophets past and present—Nathan, Isaiah of the Restoration—opposed the building of a temple.
4. The basis of a restored community is not a place of worship, but a new heart.

There are other reasons which the group might list.

After that side of the problem has been examined, turn it around and explore the other side. What are the factors which support the building of the temple? Some of them are the same as arguments against a temple:

1. Prophets past and current expected or urged the building: Ezekiel, Haggai, Zechariah.
2. The previous temple was central in the life of the people.
   a. It served as a religious symbol of their oneness.
   b. They had a place to go where they knew they might encounter God.
3. It would get the people out of their preoccupation with themselves and their own houses.
4. A place to worship would be crucial for them to function as a people of God.

As the group lists statements for and against the building of a temple, individuals may want to look carefully at the statements. Some of them will be reasons explicitly stated in the case. Others, however, may not arise from the case at all or only implicitly so. For example, the case does not say that the temple would be a heavy financial burden. That may be implied, although not necessarily. Nor does the case say that the community needed a place to come together in order that they might go out in mission. Many of the statements that are not reflected directly in the case are closely related to our values and the liabilities and assets that we attach to our own church buildings. Hence these are important statements to build on as we move the discussion from Israel to us.

B. Personal sacred space. It is often beneficial to look at our own experience in order to better understand the idea of "sacred space." Ask each individual to move back into her or his own past to recall a place that was sacred. That does not necessarily mean one's favorite church. It refers to a place, any space, where one could go and meet God. It might be a childhood memory of a spot in the woods or in the yard. It might be a spot where an adult goes to get away and be with him or herself and with God.

As individuals share their experiences of sacred space, it

may awaken the memory of others. However, there will be some people who can recall no such experience. Hearing the value that particular places have for some people may be important for those who have no such "sacred space." On the other hand, it can be instructive for others who have places which are very prominent in their ongoing religious experience to see that there are others for whom such a "place" is not essential. In previous discussions of the case this has often been one of the most powerful learnings from the dialog. It has assisted a person in understanding the differing attitude of others toward church buildings.

C. The decision to rebuild. It may be that the group members do not know that the Jews decided to rebuild the temple. In that case, the discussion might proceed with the question: Do you think that they should or should not build the temple? What are your reasons? How do you respond to the reasons on the other side?

However, many of the people will know that the temple was built. It was finished and consecrated in the spring of 515 B.C. The discussion can then move on the basis of that knowledge. Was the decision of the Jewish community to build the temple a wise one? Earlier the group outlined the reasons for and against building the temple. Which of these reasons are most persuasive as far as you are concerned?

At this point the discussion can and often naturally does turn to consider the assets and liabilities of our own church buildings. To what extent are the same assets and liabilities of "sacred space" present in our church buildings? Can we do without our own permanent sanctuary? In what way does our wider mission suffer because of the resources we put into maintaining a building? In what ways is our work energized by having our own building? How can we maximize the assets and minimize the liabilities of having sacred space? Dream a bit on how the church could organize without so much investment in buildings if in fact that is desirable.

D. Prophets on each side. One element in this case that often comes up is the problem of prophetic words speaking in favor of opposite sides of the issue. On one side there were Haggai and Zechariah urging that the temple be rebuilt. They were announcing words from Yahweh on this matter. On the other side another prophet who was active at this time, called here Isaiah of the Restoration, proclaimed a message from God. This message opposed the building of the temple. So how are these two sides to be put together? Why is it that both prophetic positions were preserved in the Bible as true?

Individual members discussing this case will seek to resolve this matter in different ways. Here are three different approaches which may arise in one form or another. Some individuals will deny that there is any opposition between the prophets. They may assert that Isaiah was not writing to the time of the Restoration but to another time. This assertion may be based on a difference of opinion among scholars. But it may also be the result of a theological necessity, namely, the confessional presupposition that nothing in the Bible could conflict in any way.

Other persons discussing this case, while admitting that there is a conflict between these prophets, may seek an overarching unity which includes both sides. A proposal for such a unity might proceed in this way: It is important to have a place to worship God as Haggai and Zechariah proclaimed, but it is also important to realize that God transcends any place, as Isaiah knew. Hence there is "truth" in both positions. A third group discussing this problem may opt for accepting the presence of both views without trying to resolve the conflict. Each prophet stated a position and the people simply had to make a decision. That is the way life is.

It is likely that other ways of responding to the issue of prophetic conflict will surface as well as different shades of the positions outlined above. If this matter surfaces early in the discussion, the group will have to decide how long to pursue it and when or whether to continue with other issues in this case.

E. Summary. Working with this case might lead the group in this manner:

1. What are the reasons against and for building a temple?
2. Do you have a "sacred space" which is meaningful to you personally?
3. Do you think that the decision to actually build the temple was a wise one? Why or why not?
4. What do you do with the fact that biblical prophets seem to differ on whether or not the temple should be built?

Concerns to Consider

As a group works with this case, there are a variety of issues which could surface. These next few paragraphs will work with only two such issues that groups have discussed in connection with this case. One is the matter of sacred space itself. The other is the matter of seemingly contradictory words from biblical prophets.

A. Sacred space. According to the biblical tradition there is no space that is sacred in and of itself. Space is sacred because people have encountered God in a particular place. Jacob's encounter with Yahweh as narrated in Genesis 28 is a good example. As a result of this meeting, Jacob sets up a stone and calls the name of that place Bethel, which means house of God. The place of encounter is not strictly a matter of human decision. The Deuteronomic tradition declares that a place becomes sacred by God's choice, "the place were Yahweh, your God, chooses to cause his name to dwell" (Deut. 12:11, 21; 14:23-24, etc.). Places are sacred because people have and do meet God there. According to the Bible, God and not the people chooses where those meeting places are. Is there any sense today in which we can say that we meet God in our sanctuaries because God chose that place?

It is not hard for us to understand that a place becomes meaningful because of an experience. This can be true for an individual or for a group. Almost all of us can recall meaningful places from childhood. It might be a spot to which we would go when there was tension in the family, or when we were lonely, or when we felt unloved or unwanted. This place might be a tree to climb, or a bush in which to hide, or even a bedroom. We could go to this place and find a measure of peace. It had become a meaningful place based on our experiences there. Can you close your eyes and take yourself to that childhood place? Can you sense the feelings you had there as a child?

Not only individuals, but groups can have experiences that cause places to be freighted with meaning. There is a group of families who return to the same camping place every year for a week. At that place they experience a unity with one another that they do not have the rest of the year even though they live in close proximity. That place has become filled with meaning on the basis of their experiences. They have tried other camping spots, but none of those seem to work. There is something about their special place that cannot be transferred.

When a space is special or sacred because an individual or a group has encountered God, then that place has become a sanctuary, a religiously sacred space. One can gain some sense of the power of the encounter with God that Israel experienced in the temple sanctuary from Psalm 24.

> Lift up your arches, O gates!
> Be raised, O ancient doors.
> So that the King of glory may enter.
> Who is this King of glory?
> Yahweh, the strong and mighty One;
> Yahweh, mighty in battle. (Ps. 24:7-8)

A sanctuary carries with it the expectation that in this place one will encounter God, because that has been the experience with the space in the past. Have you had such an experience? How would you describe such an encounter with God? How did the place play a role in the encounter?

Problems arise around sacred space. People can develop an attachment for special places that can be detrimental to their life and faith. Jeremiah denounced Israel for one kind of special attachment to the temple.

> Do not trust in hollow words by reciting,
>> "This is the temple of Yahweh,
>>> the temple of Yahweh,
>>> the temple of Yahweh." (Jer. 7:4)

Because they had experienced God's presence in the temple, Israel had come to count on that always being the case. The people thought they could always go to the temple, experience God's presence, and receive God's protection. There is no guarantee. A place is a sanctuary because God causes his name to be there. God can also withdraw from a place and then it is no longer "sacred space."

There is a second kind of detrimental attachment. Because they have experienced God in one place, people may act as if Yahweh is place-bound. If the people are forced to leave that place, then they will be cut off from God. Israel experienced this when the Babylonian Exile cut them off from Jerusalem: "How can we sing Yahweh's song in a foreign land?" (Ps. 137:4).

We, too, experience place boundness with intensity. A young bank employee felt some of this anguish. Although he and his family had moved to Chicago some years earlier, Chicago remained a foreign land: "There is no place here that is meaningful. We just want to go home to the places and the people we know." An elderly woman who had been active in church all her life quit going after she moved to a retirement home in a new community: "I can't seem to worship any place but home. God just isn't here in this new place." Places can feel so meaningful, spaces so sacred, that no place else will suffice.

There is a third way in which attachment to a sacred place

may be detrimental. Rather than empowering groups for their work, a sacred place can use up energy and resources that could be spent in other ways. Isaiah of the Restoration (Isaiah 61, quoted in Luke 4) declared that the primary work of the people of God is to bring good news to the afflicted, to bring healing to those whose lives have been broken, to proclaim freedom to those who are captive, etc. Many congregations spend so much money servicing their sacred space that they do not have the resources to reach out beyond that building. This can hit small churches especially hard. After they pay the costs of maintaining their building and a minimal level of pastoral leadership, they find that there are no financial resources left. Because of the few people involved, even the time which is available to the members can seem to be eaten up just to keep the program running in the church building itself. Bringing good news to the afflicted beyond the membership of the congregation may be lost in the process. Obviously the same thing can happen to large churches. They may have more time and money to spend, but they too can spend a large portion of it on their "temple" and its maintenance.

Sacred space brings with it both promise and problems. There is the promise that here is a place where one can meet God and receive all the strength and joy of such an encounter. That encounter may energize persons for the work and service of God's world. Sacred space also brings with it problems. People develop attachments to a place which can be limiting. Groups have special problems because one person's sacred space may seem very ordinary to another individual. That is to say, a place that is meaningful to one person may not be at all special to another. A parent may cut down a bush not knowing what it meant as a "hiding" place to his or her child. A youth group may unroll sleeping bags on the floor of a church sanctuary and run into the wrath of many who see that as desecrating their sacred space. How can we maximize the benefits and minimize the detriments of sacred space?

B. Conflict between prophets. We often assume that in previous generations decision-making was easier. The problems were less complex and the solutions clearer. Many times Christians conclude that so-called "biblical times" were the easiest moments in terms of decision-making. Not only were problems less complex and reasonable answers more clear, but the "prophets" were around to make absolutely clear what God wanted the people to do. It may be that Israel chose not to do what they knew was correct, but in those centuries there was never any doubt about what the right action was.

Certainly some things have changed to make decision-making more difficult. We have problems which seem to defy any reasonable solution, for example, when to withdraw the life support system from a terminally ill individual. Nevertheless we need to be cautious about assuming that our ancestors, even in "biblical times," had it so much easier than we do.

The process of decision-making has never been easy. It has always been difficult to decide what is beneficial and what is detrimental. Even ancient Israel and the early church struggled to know what God wanted them to do. Israel did not have only one prophet whose word on a particular matter they could either accept or reject. Rather there were many prophets speaking out at a given moment. The people had to decide which prophetic word they would follow.

In many cases the biblical tradition has separated the true and the false prophets. Even though the people at that time may not have been sure whether Hananiah or Jeremiah was the true prophet, the literature which has been preserved makes clear that Jeremiah was the true prophet (see Jer. 28). Similarly, the text in I Kings 22 states that Micaiah ben Imlah was the true prophet and Zedekiah and the four hundred prophets of the Lord were lying.

However, sometimes the biblical texts let the announcements of the prophets stand side by side even though they speak different words to the same situation. Such seems to be the case with these words from Isaiah of the post-exilic restoration and Haggai and Zechariah (Isa. 66:1, Hag. 1:4-9).

Admittedly this case involves historical reconstruction and is therefore subject to differing interpretation. It is based on the proposal of Paul D. Hanson who has worked in detail on the post-exilic centuries in his book *The Dawn of Apocalyptic.* However, even if this particular proposal should one day seem unlikely, the problem of conflicting prophetic words would not be eliminated. We have Micah saying in 725 B.C. that Jerusalem would soon be destroyed (Mic. 3:12), and Isaiah of Jerusalem saying at the same time that even though Judah will be punished, Zion will stand firm (Isa. 10:27b-34). At the same time that Jeremiah was announcing the end of Judah and Jerusalem, Habakkuk was declaring that Yahweh would intervene in behalf of those who persisted in faithful obedience. We cannot escape the fact that the Bible preserves words from prophets delivered to the same historical moment. At times these prophetic words do not mesh together easily.

As mentioned above, some people will need to deny any conflict between the canonical prophets. Their confessional position will not allow such tension in the Bible. (For more on this see the case study, **The Role of Moses,** under "Concerns to Consider.") For others it is freeing to see that the people of God have always had to make decisions between different positions, both of which are attractive.

We can look at some of our problems and not be overwhelmed by the fact that the church seems to speak with different voices. Some Christian groups speak prophetically against the proliferation of nuclear electric power plants. They declare that we are setting ourselves up for inevitable disaster either from accidents at power plants or from nuclear waste disposal. Other Christian groups are equally convinced that nuclear energy is appropriate at least as an intermediate step between fossil fuels and solar or other nonexpendable energy sources. They announce dire consequences if we do not supplement our current electrical resources with nuclear power. Abortion, disarmament, and scientific experiments with the DNA molecule are other issues on which various church groups speak conflicting prophetic words.

We are inclined to treat the conflicting words we hear from the church today in terms of true and false prophets. Sometimes that is the case, but perhaps not all conflicts can be dismissed that easily. It may be that some conflicting views need to stand side by side without quick resolution. Could it be that both Isaiah and Haggai/Zechariah had a true word from Yahweh about the temple? Is it possible that both sides on issues such as nuclear power plants and abortion have a true word to speak?

Resources to Read
Isaiah 66:1-16; Haggai 1:1-11; 2:1-19

Haggai declared what Yahweh requires: The people should go to the hills, gather wood, and build a temple in order that the glory of Yahweh may again be present in Israel. A word from Yahweh announced by Isaiah of the Restoration proclaims: Yahweh needs no "House." What God wants are humble and contrite people.

Herrmann, Siegfried. *A History of Israel in Old Testament Times.* Philadelphia: Fortress Press, 1973. Pp. 298-306.

Immediately connected with the return of the people from the Babylonian Exile is the question of the rebuilding of the temple. From Haggai and Zechariah we can conclude that the delay in rebuilding the temple was not caused by a lack of material or labor, but a lack of will to get on with the work.

Hanson, Paul D. *The Dawn of Apocalyptic.* Philadelphia: Fortress Press, 1975. Pp. 161-86.

In Israel we see a major conflict between a prophetic group with one vision of what the restored nation should be and a priestly group with a different perspective. The prophetic group was heir to Isaiah of the Exile, for whom the temple played virtually no part in the hoped-for restoration. The priestly group was heir to Ezekiel (chapters 40–48), for whom the temple was central.

Clements, R. E. *God and Temple*. Philadelphia: Fortress Press, 1965.

From her patriarchal ancestors Israel learned to understand divine presence as a personal covenant within a community. From the Canaanite religion, Israel learned to understand divine presence in specific places. Both of these contributed something to Israel's religious growth.

3.

Free at Last

Introduction

A young woman snapped: "Life at our house is so tight, so bound up that I can't breathe. With both Mom and Dad working, I have to get up and go to school when Dad leaves for work. And Dad even has to go early because my brother has band rehearsal. Mom waits and takes my sister to school later, but that's too late for me. I have to come home when Mom can come after us or hitch a ride with someone. We have to eat at exactly the same time every night because of evening plans. Mom won't let me be late and fix my own meal because my tastes don't agree with her idea of a proper diet. Then there is the house rule about how late I can be out. I can't breathe!"

A pastor in a large suburban church laments: "We have nothing but chaos. Everybody is running around doing whatever they want. There is a group who is interested in new forms of worship. Their service is at 9:00 on Sunday morning. Then the 'traditionalists' meet at 10:30. They are mad if the previous group doesn't have their clutter out of the sanctuary. Then there are the 'charismatics' who meet Sunday night. They object to the 'humanistic' youth meetings that are going on at the same time. The youth laugh at them. I have to find some way to get these groups together so that we can have some order in this madness."

The balance between order and freedom is very delicate. Too much order is stifling; too much freedom results in chaos. Finding this balance was among the problems of the young Christian community at Corinth. This was a church of first generation Christians. These Christians had been living in the ordered Greco-Roman society. Some groups within that society were assigned roles that were stiflingly structured. Such was the case with the economic and social role assigned to slaves in the Roman world. The same was true of the social and religious role assigned to women in the Jewish synagogue. The gospel provided freedom from bondage. This freedom soon resulted in conflict in the Corinthian Christian community.

The Case Study

A slave who is called in the Lord, is the Lord's free person. Likewise, the free person who has been called, is the slave of Christ. You have been bought and paid for, so do not become slaves of other people. (I Cor. 7:22-23)

There is neither Jew nor Greek, neither slave nor free, neither male and female; for all are one in Christ Jesus. (Gal. 3:28)

The Church at Corinth had heard Paul proclaim the message of freedom. In Christ Jesus there was no bondage to the roles and structures of this world, "For the form of this world is passing away" (I Cor. 7:31b). They were free at last.

This message gave freedom and new power to different groups of people. One such group was the slaves in the Roman world. Most of the slaves were either captives of war or debtors. In some of the other religions of the Roman world there were rites of freedom. Slaves could buy their freedom by selling themselves to a god or goddess. In Christ this freedom was not something one could purchase, but a free gift. Slaves began to exercise their newly received power in their lives, both inside and outside the Corinthian church.

Another group for whom Paul's message meant new power was women. Again the church seemed to be in step with the movement of the time. There was a discernible movement toward equality between male and female in the Greco-Roman culture. In Christ, the women of the church had received new freedom in worship. They became leaders in prayer and prophecy in the Corinthian church. They had the right to speak as they felt led, the freedom to dress as they chose.

However, the unqualified exercise of newly received power was causing problems. The slave in the Roman Empire had had no right of choice over what he or she would do. Slaves were to do whatever their master directed. Problems developed when slaves simply stopped fulfilling their assigned role and began exercising the power to decide what they would and would not do. The results were potentially explosive for the Christian group at Corinth.

The problems created by the women were not potential, they were already present. As women exercised their gift of freedom, the former orderliness of the worship services was lost. There was no control over the prophesying and speaking in tongues. Some women were dressing in ways that society equated with being of no account or of questionable reputation. For example, they were leaving their heads uncovered in worship. This raised confusion in the area of marriage customs. They left their heads uncovered, yet they were married. What did marriage really mean to them?

Paul had worked about a year and a half in assisting the formation of the Christian community at Corinth. Paul had not established a crisply organized institution. A highly structured organization was not his understanding of what it meant to be the body of Christ. The community at Corinth was more an organism than an organization. Now the community was trying to work out its life together. Paul had preached freedom, and he would stand by that message. This freedom was concrete. It was not just "spiritual" freedom.

Slaves and women were two quite different groups. But one thing they had in common was a new power because of their freedom in Christ. However, as they exercised their freedom, the current order of life and worship was disrupted.

Paul responded to the situation in the community at Corinth:

Everyone should remain in the state in which he or she was called. Were you a slave when called? Never mind. Even if you gain your freedom, remain in the situation you are now in. For the one who was called in the Lord as a slave is the Lord's free person. Likewise, the free person who has been called is the slave of Christ. You have been bought and paid for, so do not become slaves of other people. Each one, brethren, should remain with God in the condition in which that one was called. (I Cor. 7:20-24)

I commend you because you remember me in everything and maintain the traditions even as I have delivered them to you. Nevertheless, I want you to know that the head of every man is Christ, the head of a woman is her husband, and the head of Christ is God. Every man who prays or prophesies with something on his head, dishonors his head. However, every woman who prays or prophesies with her head uncovered, dishonors her head, for she is just like one whose head is shaved. For if a woman is uncovered, she might as well have her hair cut. But since it is disgraceful for a woman to have her hair cut or shaved, then let her cover herself. . . . But if anyone is inclined to be contentious [about this], we recognize no other custom, nor do the churches of God. (I Cor. 11:2-6, 16)

Paul directed both groups to maintain specific social roles and behavior patterns. The slaves were not to take it upon themselves to radically alter their economic situation. The women were not to change certain accepted patterns of dress.

Communiqué to Learners and Teachers

Directions for Discussion

A. *Exploring Paul's options.* This case states the reply which Paul made in responding to the difficulty in the Corinthian Church. However, we may be sure that his response was not the only one which was available. As we involve ourselves in the situation, let us consider what options were available to Paul. Understanding of the case will be facilitated if the class first gets before it a list of all the options that group members can think of. Some of the more obvious ones include:

1. Stay out of controversy.
2. Explain what he meant by freedom.
3. Support the slaves and women.

There are many more. There need not be any attempt to evaluate the options suggested by individuals at this point. It is sufficient just to list them.

Having listed all of the possibilities which come to mind, look again at what Paul did. How would you describe his response? Certainly he did not choose to "Stay out of the controversy." Nor can we say that he chose to "Explain what he meant by freedom." Paul gives no generalized explanation about what freedom means and what the limitations on freedom might be. He might have limited freedom to a strictly personal inner experience as opposed to an external, concrete change. But Paul did not generalize in this way. How can we characterize Paul's response?

The next step in exploring Paul's options might be to look at the advantages and disadvantages of the response Paul made. In our own lives, we know that even the decision to intervene in a controversy has advantages and disadvantages, regardless of the nature of our intervention. For example, when parents see children arguing or fighting, they have to decide whether or not to intervene. The advantages to stepping into children's disputes include: teaching them how to handle fights and resolve conflicts, preventing the fight from going so far that someone gets hurt, and restoring "peace and quiet" to the home as quickly as possible. However, there are disadvantages to such intervention also. Children need to learn to settle their own disputes without outside interference. The parent will likely end up having one or both sides mad at him or her. The parent may not really know what the problem is and thus try to settle things on the basis of wrong information. Regardless of the way in which parents step into a dispute between siblings, the act of stepping in has pros and cons.

So it is with Paul's decision in the Corinthian Church controversy. Paul decided to step in and he chose to intervene in a specific way. What risks did Paul take? What might he have gained or lost?

B. From Corinth to us. As we are describing the situation at Corinth and the nature of Paul's response, what he might gain or lose, we inevitably begin to bring our own experience to bear on the situation. That is certainly appropriate. How do we view what Paul did? Is there an option among those listed previously that seems more beneficial than the one Paul chose? As the group pursues this question, at least two different aspects might be discussed.

One is the fact of Paul's intervention. Was Paul acting paternalistically in his intervention, as a parent would treat children? Paternalism currently has negative connotations. There are many reasons for this. It implies that a person is treating other adults as if they were children. This assumption of "superiority" may have no basis in reality. Further, paternalism can hinder the growth and maturity of other people if a pater-type steps in and shows them what to do or settles their disputes. Christian mission work has often been accused of indulging in paternalism which is harmful to the maturation of churches in non-Western cultures. Perhaps Paul's intervention was not paternalistic in this negative way. It may have been an appropriate intervention. What are the marks of appropriate and inappropriate intervention in a group by a powerful figure? Where have we seen beneficial ways of intervening? Where have we seen harmful interference?

A second aspect that might be pursued is the nature of Paul's intervention. For this we need to refer back to the characterization of Paul's message, and the advantages and disadvantages of his response. Paul did not retract his fundamental message of freedom. Nor did he write Corinth an essay on the nature of freedom. On the other hand, he did give advice (or lay down a directive) on these particular cases. In both cases he directed that Corinth follow the social customs of that time. This response by Paul might be probed in a number of ways. Here is a list of questions which might facilitate the discussion. They all move in somewhat the same direction, but some groups get a "handle" on the issues involved more easily with one question than another.

1. We often talk at length about the nature of freedom and its limits. Paul apparently did not do this. Would it have been helpful if he had? Why or why not?

2. The limits to freedom were settled on a case by case basis by Paul at Corinth. Is that an adequate way to proceed? Should we seek some general rules applicable in all cases? What might they be?

3. In these two cases when the freedom of the gospel collided with custom, Paul supported custom. Is that always what we are to do? When should freedom enable Christians to break through the constraints of custom?

As the group discusses this, people will likely mention current situations in which the issue of freedom and order arises. For example, the need for freedom inevitably conflicts with order in the family. To allow it to function, a family must have some order. Hence most families have customary times for meals. These mealtimes have been established over the long period of time as the family grew into a cohesive unit. Another custom that many families have involves appropriate clothing for different activities. Again this is seldom a matter of conscious decision. It just "is" that way.

One of the essential elements in the maturing of young adults is that they be given "freedom." Very often their exercise of freedom will cause a collision with the family "order." An after-school job, sport, or music activity may conflict with the only meal that the family customarily eats together. Current dress fashions among young adults regularly are at odds with the expectations of their parents.

1. Should these conflicts be decided on a case by case basis? Are there general rules which limit freedom?
2. When should freedom be allowed to break through custom? When should order be upheld as a limitation on freedom?
3. By whom and how should these questions be settled?

C. Summary. A class discussion using this case might move in the following way:

1. What options might Paul have had in responding to the Corinthian conflict?
2. How would you describe what Paul did?
3. What are the advantages and disadvantages of the response Paul made?
4. What do you think and feel about Paul's action?
   a. Should he have intervened?
   b. Was his response adequate?
5. Where do we see communities wrestling with conflict between freedom and order?

Concerns to Consider

Group discussion surfaces different issues in this case. There are two that frequently capture the attention of the discussants. One issue involves the exercise of power by community leaders. In this case it is Paul who exerts power within the community. The second issue is very closely related to this one. It pertains to the relationship between order in the community and the freedom of individual community members. With no thought that these exhaust the issues in this case, let us focus on these two.

By virtue of their position in the community, leaders have a certain amount of power. The amount of power and the way that power is obtained differs from one community to another. Paul's power in the church at Corinth had to do with his role as "founder" of that particular community. Although he was no longer present, he kept in touch with the Corinthians and still possessed at least some power to influence the life of that community.

Issues surrounding the use and misuse of power and the gaining and losing of power are complex. One factor which enters into the use of power by the leadership is the goal toward which the power is directed. Leaders may exercise power for their own benefit, to keep themselves in power, or for their personal profit. Secondly, power may be exercised in behalf of a particular group within the community. A member of Congress may exercise power in behalf of "special interest groups." The mayor of a town may push things in such a way as to benefit "cronies." Finally, power may be used to benefit the community as a whole. Certainly this latter one is generally accepted as the best goal. In practice the power exercised by community leadership generally is a mixture of all three, that is, of benefit to the leader, selected people, and the community as a whole. We might ask whether Paul was exercising power for his own benefit, in behalf of those he liked best in the community, or in the interest of the community as a whole. We have little information by which to answer the question of Paul's motives, but it is worth raising for us.

Having said that it is best to exercise power for the benefit of the whole community, we are still left with a multitude of problems. One of these is especially clear in this case. How does the leader of the community balance the need for order in the community with the need for freedom? The slaves and women had been freed through Paul's preaching. Their freedom had to be protected. On the other hand, the exercise of that freedom was creating disorder, especially in the economic sphere and in worship services. Certainly, a community needs a degree of order or it will cease to be a community. But when does the demand for order become excessive?

Virtually every leader has to work at this problem. Think about the administrator of a retirement home. The residents of the home need freedom to live to their fullest potential, whether they be bedridden or ambulatory, mentally alert or with declining mental faculties. However, for the retirement home to be life-enhancing for anyone, there must be some order in that community. It is up to the leadership of the community to find a balance which is most beneficial. Retirement and nursing homes vary widely in the balance between freedom and order which the leadership effects.

Even the leadership of a corporation has to work with this matter. The president of a small electronics corporation stated the obvious. The goal of his corporation was to make a profit. In order to accomplish that goal, he needed an efficiently ordered operation. However, if he erred too much on the side of tight order, he would end up with unhappy employees who would quit whenever they could. Rapid turnover of employees would have the effect of reducing efficiency and would greatly diminish his chances of making a corporate profit. Thus he had to find ways to allow a certain amount of freedom to individuals even if this created a degree of disorder. The president was conducting a series of seminars for interested employees to enable them to find ways to express their freedom, to reach their own goals, to be themselves within the ordered corporate structure of that electronics firm.

The discussion earlier about the family points to the same issue. For a family to be a functioning unit, there needs to be a certain amount of order: times to eat, procedures for getting work done, generally accepted behavioral norms. If all order collapses, the family falls apart. Yet the individuals within the family need freedom to grow in their own individuality, to act in ways that are appropriate to their own character and moment in their life pilgrimage. Where is the balance between the two? What is the role of parental leadership in maintaining that balance?

What are the marks of a community that has a good balance between freedom and order? Can you think of leaders that facilitate or hinder that balance?

Resources to Read

I Corinthians 7:17-24; 11:2-16

Paul advised everyone to lead the life which the Lord has assigned to that person. At the same time Paul admonished the Corinthians not to become slaves of other people because they were free in the Lord.

Bartchy, S. Scott. *First-Century Slavery and I Corinthians 7:21* (SBL Dissertation Series 11). Missoula, Montana: The Society of Biblical Literature, 1973. Pp. 37-40.

Slavery in the Greek and Roman world was not the same as the picture we have of the American experience. Under certain conditions slaves could work independently and own property. Nevertheless the slave was characterized by total powerlessness over his or her own life. The situation was as tolerable as the master chose to make it.

Scroggs, Robin. "Paul and the Eschatological Woman." *Journal of the American Academy of Religion* 40 (September, 1972). Pp. 283-303 (especially 289-91, 297-303).

In different parts of the Roman world women were treated in various ways. In Egypt, they had a great deal of autonomy. One of the most restrictive groups was traditional Judaism. It was from the synagogue that many of the early Christians came. Paul is clear in wanting freedom for women in the Christian community.

Barrett, C. K. *The First Epistle to the Corinthians*. New York: Harper & Row, 1968. Pp. 1-27.

The new city of Corinth was built by Julius Caesar in about 44 B.C. While it had a proverbial reputation for vice, it was likely no better or worse than other seaport towns. Paul's relationship with the Corinthian church as portrayed in his letters was a stormy one, including moments of real love and intense anger.

4.

The Role of Moses

Introduction

We live in a time of liberation movements. The current wave of such movements in the United States began with the black liberation movement which was most prominent during the 1960s. Presently there are several such movements going on simultaneously. Women, Native Americans, and various ethnic, racial, and national groups are seeking release from the constraints of our social, political, and economic systems. We are constantly faced with the question of how to be related to such movements. A number of things govern our decision. We cannot be related to everything, so we are selective. We eliminate some freedom efforts because it is not practical for us to be actively related to them. We say no to others because we do not agree with their goals.

While we can be selective to some degree, there are particular freedom movements and specific moments in which we find ourselves compelled to be involved. Circumstances may place us right in the middle of a situation of racial or age discrimination. When this is combined with an inner feeling or Christian commitment which calls us to be involved, the result is that we are personally related to a freedom movement.

However, that still leaves open the "how" of our relationship to the particular freedom movement.

Such a question faced a couple whom we shall call Sally and Ed Reeves. They found out that a black family wished to buy the house two doors down from them. The realtor would not sell it to the black family. Legally, it was difficult to show that it was a case of racial discrimination, but it seemed that way to the Reeves. They then had to decide how to involve themselves. They might sign the petition that was coming around supporting the black family. This signed petition was to be published in the paper. The Reeves might even take the petition around themselves. There were still other ways in which they could become involved. Circumstances forced involvement. At the very least, the Reeves had to decide whether or not to sign the petition. The only question remaining was the role that they were to play in this freedom movement both individually and together.

Exodus is probably the most familiar freedom story in the Bible. We learned the story from childhood, discussed it in study groups, and heard it used in the pulpit. The drama begins by relating that it was only by the grace of God that there was a Moses to lead the people to freedom. Many of us have wished that we could hear our calling with as much clarity as Moses seemed to hear his. However, we can also identify with Moses' reluctance to get involved.

This case centers in on the leadership role Moses was to take in the Exodus. As we will see when we look at the biblical texts carefully, this is not a role that can be easily explained. We say that Moses was the leader, but that does not answer all the questions. The Exodus was God's freedom movement, not Moses'. So biblically it is more accurate to say that God was the leader. That being the case, what was Moses' role?

God's action in the world has always been a freedom movement. Hopefully we can better understand our roles in God's freedom movement by exploring the role of Moses in the Exodus.

The Case Study

Yahweh said [to Moses], "I have seen the affliction of my people who are in Egypt, and I have heard their anguished cries on account of their slave masters. I know their pain. Hence I have come down to deliver them from the hand of the Egyptians and to bring them up from this land. . . . Indeed the anguished cry of the people of Israel has come to me, and I have seen the oppression with which the Egyptians oppress them. So now, I send you to Pharaoh to deliver my people, Israel, from Egypt. (Exod. 3:7-10)

Moses had seen the intolerable conditions of the Hebrews in Egypt. Although he was not personally a victim of the oppression, he knew the suffering of his people and acted on behalf of them, creating a situation which forced him to flee Egypt.

One day, Moses . . . went out to his people. He saw their burdens, and he noticed an Egyptian beating a Hebrew, one of his brothers. He looked around carefully and seeing no one, killed the Egyptian and buried him in the sand. (Exod. 2:11-12)

Working in exile as a herdsman, Moses had an experience which convinced him that God also knew the conditions of the Hebrews in Egypt. Furthermore God told him that events were coming in which God would act to free the people. The oppressed Israelites would be given a place to live where they would not be in bondage. Moses perceived that the deliverance day was at hand.

Moses as Messenger

Moses, himself, had a role to play in this developing drama. He was to be God's messenger.

Go, gather the leaders of Israel and say to them, "Yahweh, the God of your ancestors, . . . appeared to me, saying, 'I am deeply concerned about you and what has been done to you in Egypt. Hence I declare that I will deliver you from Egypt. . . .' " (Exod. 3:16-17)

The word from God which Moses experienced was typical of the calling of a messenger. Such speeches regularly began with an instruction: "Go . . . and say." As was customary, the messenger was then given a speech to deliver. He was to tell the people that God was about to act on their behalf, to deliver them from bondage.

Moses was called to be God's messenger. A messenger's role was clearly defined in that day. Kings had messengers. It was through the messenger that the king informed others about what he was going to do. Through a messenger a king could declare war or ask for peace, negotiate trade or renew friendship. Through Moses, Yahweh announced to the people of Israel that God was coming to deliver them from the hand of Pharaoh.

Moses as Servant

"So now I send *you* to Pharaoh *to deliver* my people, Israel, from Egypt" (Exod. 3:10, *italics mine*). Send Moses to deliver? That was *not* the role of a messenger. A messenger would be sent to announce what the king—God—was doing. If there was any *delivering* to be done, the king, not the messenger, would do it.

However, in this text Moses was directed to be the one who brought the people out of bondage. This was much closer to the role of a servant. The servant was the one who acted on behalf of the master. To be sure, the servant was "sent" by the master. The work that the servant was to do was the work of the master. The servant was under "orders" and had no choice in the work that was to be done. Nevertheless the servant's active role was different from that of the messenger. So the verse just quoted portrays Moses in a different role as one sent "to deliver my people, Israel, from Egypt." There are two texts which preserve two different statements of Moses' role. Moses, the messenger of Yahweh; Moses, the servant of Yahweh. The messenger was the one through whom the king announced what he was about to do. The servant was the one through whom a master's work was accomplished.

Communiqué to Learners and Teachers

Directions for Discussion

This case as it is presented is not primarily directed toward the Exodus as an event. Rather it directs our attention to significant aspects of the event as portrayed in the text itself. In the Exodus account we find the role of Moses described in two different ways, the messenger role and the servant role. The suggestions for discussing the case will proceed with that focus.

A. *Messenger or servant.* One way to begin the discussion of this case is to encourage the class to be clear about some similarities and differences between the messenger and the servant as they are described in this case. A listing of similarities might include the following:

1. Both are working for another person.
2. Both the servant and messenger had clear "orders."
3. In this case they are both sent to do their work in another locale.
4. The result of the work is the same; people are freed.

The group will mention other similarities.

The corresponding task is to enumerate some differences between the two roles. Again there are many possibilities. Here are some that have been frequently mentioned.

Messenger	Servant
1. Spokesperson for God	1. Agent of God
2. Goes to leaders of Israel	2. Goes to Pharaoh
3. God delivers	3. Moses delivers

It is beneficial to get some general agreement on the similarities and differences between Moses as messenger and Moses as servant at the beginning. This enables the group to move on to other questions.

B. *The New Testament portrait of Jesus.* We might first look at the way in which Jesus embodied these two roles. Can we talk about Jesus as a messenger? Certainly Jesus as the one who announced the coming of the kingdom of God is central to the New Testament. Among other places, a portrait of Jesus as teacher-announcer is important to the Gospel of Matthew. In the role of a servant, Jesus as the one through whom deliverance is accomplished is crucial to Christian theology. For example, Jesus Christ as the "way" to freedom is significant in the Gospel of John.

The so-called "inaugural address" of Jesus which is found in Luke 4:18-19 lifts up both Jesus as proclaimer of freedom and agent of deliverance.

"The Spirit of the Lord is upon me,
because he has anointed me to *preach* good news to the poor.
He has sent me to *proclaim* release to the captives
and recovery of sight to the blind,
to *set at liberty* those who are oppressed,
to *proclaim* the acceptable year of the Lord." (Luke 4:18-19, *italics mine.*)

C. The church as messenger and servant. The task now becomes to explore the ways in which these two roles might translate into our experience. Most Christians would agree that the mission of the church is to be related in some way with the deliverance which God is effecting in the world. Whether the bondage be physical and material or spiritual and psychological, the Christian message is one of freedom. Can the roles of messenger and servant help us understand ways in which we can be related to God's freedom movement?

Usually the discussion of this case is directed quite naturally toward a congregation's understanding of its mission. Where can we see the role of messenger and servant visible in congregational life and organization? Among the areas of church life and organization that have been explored in discussions of this case are:

1. Relief and rehabilitation work, e.g. Church World Service, International Conference of Catholic Charities.

2. Social and political action, e.g. Friends' Committee on National Legislation, Southern Christian Leadership Conference.
3. Evangelistic and revival meetings.
4. The counseling ministry.
5. The sermon.

There are many others that might be mentioned. It will certainly be the case that not every function of the church can be neatly divided into these two roles. Which tasks have aspects of both the messenger role and the servant role? Are there some which fit into neither category?

It is often helpful to share with one another how we evaluate ourselves and our congregation in relationship to the role of messenger and servant. Do I feel myself more comfortable in one role than the other? Do I feel that one of the roles is more important or more appropriate for a Christian than the other? Is one of the roles emphasized more than the other in our congregation? Does our historical moment need more messengers proclaiming God's deliverance or more servants doing the work?

Some congregations find themselves deeply divided over whether they should be messengers or servants. One such congregation is described in a case entitled "Operation Reach-Out." This congregation was split over a proposal that they take a zealous "messenger" type stance to the mission of the church, i.e., that they go throughout the neighborhood talking to individuals about the gospel. A group might be interested in discussing that case as a follow-up to this one. A copy of "Operation Reach-Out" may be obtained from Intercollegiate Case Clearing House, Soldiers Field, Boston, Massachusetts 02163.

D. Two pictures in one text. This case also gives a group the opportunity to wrestle with the process through which the Bible was shaped and finally written and the implications which that has for the authority of the Bible. How does one explain the fact that within one text there are two different portrayals of Moses' relationship to the Exodus? Although there are many similarities between the roles of messenger and servant, they are not the same. Especially important is the question of whether Moses was actually the "deliverer" or whether he announced that God would deliver.

Some persons choose to work at an explanation within the understanding that the Exodus account was written by a single author, Moses. How can this view explain the two different roles given Moses in the same text?

The single-author theory might argue that the two roles are not really different, that the similarities far outweigh the differences. One would then proceed with a process of harmonization. This involves making the differences fit together so that the conflict is only apparent and the reality a single, unified picture.

Another approach within the single-author theory is that God wanted to teach us that these two roles really belong together. The church needs both messengers and servants. With this interpretation Exodus 3 is understood to have a message similar to that in I Corinthians 12:14—"The body does not consist of one member but of many." Hence some are called to be messengers, others are chosen for the servant role, but all are one. God directed that the account be written in this way in order to make this point.

Other persons see development of the Pentateuch (Genesis, Exodus, Leviticus, Numbers, and Deuteronomy) not in terms of God's revelation to a single author, but as God's working through the processes of history. God worked in and through the lives of a people and out of their life together the Bible emerged. How might this explain the tension in the text?

One possibility is to describe the tension in the text as an emergent process. The story of Moses and the Exodus was told in different places, perhaps at different sanctuaries. In one place the role of Moses was described in messenger terms. Among another group the role was that of a servant. As the people moved about, gradually these stories with slight variations merged into one. However, the slight differences in the accounts were not lost; the narrative that emerged from this process preserved a picture of Moses as both messenger and servant in the drama.

Other people may describe this merging of different stories as a literary process. At one time there were two different written accounts of the Exodus. In one account Moses was understood as a messenger. In the other account Moses was portrayed as a servant. In the final editing, both pictures were preserved. Hence the final version was not a rewriting of the Exodus account so much as a splicing of the two accounts together.

The group discussing this issue may have variations on the proposals outlined above or perhaps entirely different suggestions. Although it is not beneficial for a case discussion to become a battle for the Bible, it can be useful to investigate and share one's own position as it encounters this particular text.

E. Summary. The flow of the discussion might go something like this:
1. What are the similarities and differences between Moses as messenger and Moses as servant?
2. Where can we see these two roles in the activities of the church?
   a. Do I see myself more as a messenger or a servant?
   b. Does the church as a whole need more emphasis on the messenger role or the servant role?
3. How do we explain the fact that two different roles for Moses are portrayed in the same biblical narrative?

Concerns to Consider

One way in which we experience the distinction between a messenger-type ministry and a servant-style ministry involves our tendency to separate "evangelism" from "social action."

This is by no means the only way a distinction might be illustrated, but it is useful as an illustration because of the tension it has caused within many groups. Other illustrations of messenger roles and servant roles can be picked up from the group's discussion and from the "Directions for Discussion." Another concern upon which this section will touch briefly is the problem of the authority of the Bible. This issue arises because of the two different portraits of Moses contained in one text.

A. Evangelism and/or Social Action. Before the discussion proceeds too far, a word needs to be said about definitions. "Evangelism" can be broadly conceived to include the entire mission of the church. It can be narrowly conceived in terms of revival meetings. In these paragraphs the word is being used somewhere in between a very broad and a very narrow definition. Evangelism here refers to an oral or written ministry of the church which aims to secure a religious decision. This may be done by public meetings and through public media such as television or it may happen on an individual basis by personal visitation. Its connection to the role of messenger is clear. Evangelism, so defined, involves *proclamation of the deliverance God will accomplish* in the lives of people. It then calls a person to act in response to that proclamation.

"Social action" is less interested in calling individuals to a religious decision in response to a presentation of what God is doing. It is more directed to *participation* in the freedom movement which God has announced. Examples of this include the black liberation movement which became involved in mass demonstrations, economic boycotts, voter registrations, and other tactics designed to free black Americans from the social and economic bondage in which they were living. A second example is the Human Equality movement which wants to effect equality for people regardless of their sex. Church denominations and congregations are deeply involved in both these movements. Certainly social action as defined here cannot be limited to what might be called liberation movements. Prison reform efforts, programs designed to deal with chemical (drug) dependency, antinuclear and clean environment campaigns are among many other things that might be described as "social action." The common factor is that the persons involved see themselves as working to free others from the bondage of social roles, political or economic systems, drugs, etc. This approach directs Christians to be involved in these activities as servants of God. God is concerned about people in bondage and *directs individuals to be the effective agents of God's deliverance.* This is obviously more closely related to the action of Moses, the servant, as this role is described in the case.

Is your congregation or denomination divided over whether evangelism or social action is what the church is called to do? Frequently congregations will have individuals pushing the group to be more active in evangelism. They push denominations to come up with evangelistic programs that are designed to "call people to Christ." At the same time other persons will press the church to get serious about delivering black Africans from the system of apartheid, electing and ordaining women to positions previously occupied only by men, effecting reform of the juvenile justice system, etc.

Many times these two groups do not like each other. The evangelistic group accuses the other group of trying to "build" the kingdom of God, of attempting to do God's work. Those inclined to social action complain that the other faction does not care about the social, political, and economic systems which enslave people. They sit waiting for God to act when God has called us to involvement.

Congregations handle this division in a number of ways. Sometimes one group chooses or is forced to leave the congregation. Often each group tries to do its own thing and stay out of the other's way. Conflict arises at congregational meetings, especially when it comes time to tackle the budget.

Very infrequently do these two groups see each other's ministry as having an indispensable role in God's freedom movement. Seeing both roles, the messenger and the servant, attributed to Moses in one text, in the retelling of one event, moves us in the direction of embracing both roles. When we recall the discussion of similarities between the servant and the messenger, we realize that both are called by the same Lord for the same goal of freedom, but through two different roles. Do you think both evangelism and social action are appropriate roles for Christians? Where have you seen these two roles working together? Where have you seen them clash?

B. Tensions in the text. This case presents an opportunity to discuss questions about consistency and hence the "truth" of the Bible. If a single text says that *God* delivered Israel from Egypt and that God sent *Moses* to deliver Israel from Egypt, can the Bible be true?

In one theological perspective the "truth" of the Bible is based on the complete consistency of all the statements in the Bible. The Bible was divinely dictated and hence is logically consistent and historically accurate in all its particulars. This position asserts that if there is any incongruity, then the Bible is not true; the Bible is fallible and hence not authoritative. To concede that Exodus 3 gives two views of the role of Moses which are not harmonious would be problematic to this position. Furthermore, the advocates of this position state that any discrepancies are only so on the surface. If one explores deeper, one finds the Bible free of "inconsistencies."

There may well be individuals in the study group who hold this position. Their perspective must be taken seriously. For these people to concede that there is an inconsistency in the text may be experienced by them as undermining the foundation of their faith. However, this ought not to keep us from exploring this text. It is a chance to listen to one another. How can we learn from and respond to those who have this view of the Bible?

For other people, the Bible can be a norm for their life and faith without the demands of absolute logical and historical consistency. The Bible was formed by the community over centuries and differences within the community and historical developments are reflected in the Bible. This does not mean it is not the work of God. God has a chosen people. The Bible is the result of God at work in and through his people. This work can be described in many ways, but this position acknowledges both elements, human and divine. God is at work, and it is a very human community through whom God works. For people holding this position, in a wide variety of forms, the fact that Moses is portrayed in two different ways in one text is not a significant problem. The truth of the Bible is defined in terms of the message of its texts to us rather than the logical consistency and historical accuracy of this living story.

Can these two views of the Bible live together in one congregation or denomination? If the discussion group is struggling with this question, it may be beneficial to go through the same process which the group used with the case. What are the similarities and differences of these two positions on the Bible? Does each of these positions have a place in the church? What can we learn from one another?

Resources to Read

Exodus 1:1-4, 17

The anguish in Egypt is dramatically portrayed. The Hebrews' life as forced laborers became bitter; finally the Hebrew midwives were directed to kill every newborn male. However, God was about to act. Moses was called to participate in God's freedom movement.

Rad, Gerhard von. *Old Testament Theology*. Vol. I. New York: Harper & Row, 1962. Pp. 289-96.

Throughout their history, Israel's theologians continued to reflect on Moses and his role in the Exodus. Was he a messenger, a prophet, a servant, a miracle worker? Moses became a crucial figure and was used to demonstrate many of the roles to which Yahweh called Israel as the people of God.

Herrmann, Siegfried. *A History of Israel in Old Testament Times.* Philadelphia: Fortress Press, 1975. Pp. 61-64.

As a historical figure, Moses emerges as an intermediary between two sides, the Egyptian state and the oppressed aliens. He had connections with both sides. Moses was a Semite with an Egyptian name and a Midianite wife.

Barr, James. *The Bible in the Modern World.* New York: Harper & Row, 1973. Or in abbreviated form "Scripture, authority of," in *The Interpreter's Dictionary of the Bible.* Supplementary Volume. Nashville: Abingdon, 1976. Pp. 794-97.

The normativeness of the Bible has been described with a number of terms such as inspiration, Word of God, authority.

The primary problem with the category of inspiration is deciding "in what way" God inspired the writing. We must assume that the "way" in which this happened is not any different than the mode in which God continues to relate to humanity.

Lindsell, Harold. *The Battle for the Bible.* Grand Rapids: Zondervan Publishing House, 1976.

The Bible is free from error in its original autographs. It is accurate in all detail regarding historical facts and doctrinal statements. Any other position leads to disaster. Although Lindsell's position obviously is not the assumption of this book, his position represents that of many church members.

Part II
Living as a People

The first group of cases concentrated on community shaping issues. Issues raised in those cases touched the organization of the people of God: their administration, customs, buildings, and mission. The cases in this section move in a different direction. Certainly they are community shaping in their own way. Any time a group wrestles with and resolves an issue, the community is thereby shaped and molded. However, while the cases in the first section tended to involve inaugural moments in the life of the community, the ones in this section do not. These cases lift up problems which arise out of the ongoing life of the community.

In this section there are again four cases. The first case, **One Nation, Two Gods,** is taken from the period of Israel's monarchy. The community of people living in the area called Israel were deeply divided by religion and to some extent by social and economic factors. As king, Omri and later Ahab were responsible for finding a way to unify this divided community. **The King and the Prophet** also takes up a moment from the same period at a time when the future existence of the people of God was very much in doubt. Israel might be destroyed by an external enemy or internal disintegration.

The third case, **The Conscience and the Community,** turns again to the Corinthian Church. Various members of that church differed in the degree to which they had become fully integrated into their new community. They had been deeply attached to other communities, and such attachments are not easily broken. The final case, **The Family and the Kingdom of God,** is similar to the **Role of Moses** in that it concentrates on a biblical text rather than a moment from the history of biblical times. This case involves a conflict in loyalty between one's responsibility to family and to the "kingdom of God."

1.

One Nation, Two Gods

Introduction

Within a family, a "division in the house" can occur over countless things. For example, on the same Friday night there were two school events asking for the presence of the Lindsay family. Aaron wanted to go to the concert, not to the basketball game: "Why go see a bunch of boys trying to get a ball through a hoop? The outcome of the game doesn't matter anyway. What do I get out of it? A headache from the noise! But music, orchestra music reaches in and moves you, calming you down or stirring you up."

"Putting me to sleep!" retorted Ellen, his sister. "The concert is nothing except boring. How can you trade that for the excitement of a close basketball game?"

Such a division is common. It is seldom overcome by persuasion, cajoling, or even force. Either Aaron or Ellen might consent to attend the other's activity, but the division would remain. While it might appear that the conflict between Aaron and Ellen is minor, it was in fact a division that arose from the heart of the personal identity of these two individuals. Music for Aaron and spectator sports for Ellen struck the very center of who they were as persons. The way out of this particular conflict was relatively easy, at least on that occasion. The two went their separate ways. However, "separate ways" is not always the best method to solve disunity.

If there are divisions in a family, the chance for division in a larger, more diverse community is that much greater. Race has been an element of fundamental disunity in the United States. It is a problem which seems to many people to defy solution. In other times and places religion has been the focus of fundamental disunity between people. For example, in Africa there are several countries in which there has been deep antagonism between Islamic and Christian communities, or between one of these and an indigenous tribal religion. Northern Ireland, the Middle East, and India have witnessed major tragedies caused by religious division.

One Nation, Two Gods focuses on the role religion played in the division which rent the Northern Kingdom of Israel in the ninth century B.C. The large Canaanite population depended on Baal to provide rain for the fields and to insure fertility for the flocks. The Israelite population turned to Yahweh as the one who had delivered them from trouble and could sustain them. Finding some way to govern this deeply divided kingdom was the dilemma that faced Omri and later his son Ahab.

The Case Study

David spoke to Yahweh:

> You delivered me during strife with the peoples,
> You established me as the head of nations,
> People that I did not know served me. (II Sam. 22:44)

The military victories of David had expanded the boundaries of Israel to include many diverse people, people who were not Hebrew, people that the Israelites "did not know."

Although the new people now under David's rule were a mixture of different ethnic and national groups, they had certain things in common. For the most part, they were merchants, crafts-people, and landowners. Another thing that these people had in common was religion. They called their principal god Baal. They believed that their very existence depended on the power of Baal, especially important was his power to produce grain in the fields and bring fertility among the flocks. A line from Canaanite poetry declared:

> For the earth, the rain of Baal,
> And for the fields, the rain of
> the Exalted Handsome One.

Both the life-giving rain and the destructive storms were believed to be controlled by Baal. The life and safety of the Canaanite people were based on their allegiance to Baal.

How should the Hebrew people relate to these newly incorporated citizens? In contrast to the more urban, landowning Canaanites, the Israelites tended to be rural townsfolk. Their identity was based on the action of Yahweh. "Yahweh brought us out of Egypt with a mighty hand and an outstretched arm, with overwhelming terror, with wondrous signs. Yahweh brought us to this place and gave us this land, a land flowing with milk and honey" (Deut. 26:8-9).

David attempted to bring all of the people together under one unified religion, centered in allegiance to Israel's God, Yahweh. "King David dedicated everything to Yahweh; the silver and gold which he took from all the nations which he conquered, from Edom, Moab, the Ammonites, the Philistines, Amalek . . ." (II Sam. 8:11-12 *adapted*). This worked during David's reign. At least he was able to hold the nation together. However, it did not solve the relationship between the Hebrews and the Canaanites for the future.

Solomon tried another approach. He encouraged the

assimilation of the two groups. He allowed the Canaanite peoples to have temples to Baal. Temples were built to Ashtoreth, the goddess of Sidon, and Milcom, the Baal of the Ammonites. "Then Solomon built a sanctuary for Chemoth, [the god] of Moab" (I Kings 11:7). Solomon also built the temple at Jerusalem to Yahweh. This was the national sanctuary. It was built to conform to the model of the temples of Baal under the direction of foreign architects. "And King Solomon sent and brought Hiram from Tyre. . . . He came to King Solomon and did all his work for him" (I Kings 7:13-14).

Solomon's effort to melt the two groups into one through accommodation and assimilation did not solve the problem. For one thing, the Hebrew belief about Yahweh made assimilation difficult. There were limits on the extent to which their religion could accommodate Baalism, e.g., "You shall have no other gods before me" (Exod. 20:3). In fact, certain groups among the Israelites urged the extermination of all non-Yahweh worshipers in accord with the tradition about Joshua. "Joshua defeated the whole land. . . . He completely destroyed everything that breathed, as Yahweh, the God of Israel, commanded" (Josh. 10:40).

The problem went unresolved for a century. Then Omri, the king of the Northern state of Israel again had to face the question: How could he make one nation out of a people having two fundamentally different identities growing out of two different religions?

Omri and his son Ahab considered another policy. They might set up separate governmental structures for each of the two groups. This would mean two separate capitals, Samaria on the historically Canaanite soil; Jezreel in the traditionally Israelite area. It would mean having two different armies and two separate sets of officials for the towns controlled by the two groups. Then the two religious groups could exist side by side in one nation, separate but equal.

This proposal, too, had no assurance of success. In fact, Elijah was sure that it would not work. "Elijah approached the people and said, 'How long will you limp along with two opinions? If Yahweh is God, follow him. If Baal, then follow him' " (I Kings 18:21). Two gods for one nation was fundamentally wrong according to Elijah. Since he considered Yahweh to be the one true God, Elijah demanded that all elements of Baalism be eliminated from the country.

Communiqué to Learners and Teachers

Directions for Discussion

A. Exploring the options. In discussing this case, it is often fruitful to begin by exploring several options which might have been available to Omri and Ahab. Some approaches to Israel's disunity have already been mentioned. These options are the ones which seem to have been used or seriously proposed during Israel's history. The attempt to create a unified religious entity could be approached in at least two different ways: assimilation or elimination. Taking elimination first: Omri might destroy one of the two groups. This is the direction which is proposed by the book of Joshua. It is also close to what Elijah calls for. With the extermination of the adherents of Baal (or Yahweh), the country would have a single religion.

Israel could move toward a single religion also by assimilation. The two groups would merge, and the resulting religion would then be a combination of the two. This appears to be the approach that Solomon took. Like elimination, the goal of assimilation is to create a unified nation with a single religion.

There are other possibilities. One might find a way to permit each of the two religious groups to exist side by side. The king would have to develop the "rules" which would enable this coexistence to function. "Majority-minority" is one working arrangement that might be tried. One group would become the majority or the powerful group. This group would be the basis of the national identity. The other group would be the minority. Their options and freedom would be determined by the majority. "Separate but equal" is another set of rules which might be tried. This arrangement would attempt to balance the two groups, seeing that each got equal treatment.

There are other possibilities which the discussion will surface. For example, Omri might give up trying to put together one nation and just allow the two peoples to go their separate ways. In summary, it is often helpful to let the group begin by listing options without initially evaluating any of the suggestions.

B. Evaluating the options. There are different ways that the group might use to evaluate the options which have been listed. In some groups it has been facilitating to begin by having individuals say which option they would erase from the list and their reason for that. Then the class members might be asked whether they agree or disagree.

Today, many discussion groups are inclined to easily dismiss the option of making Israel a one-God nation by exterminating one of the two religious groups. It is important to remember that this was the position of the book of Joshua, the book of Kings, in which the reigns of Omri and Ahab are described, and also of the prophet Elijah.

Soon the discussion will probably switch from the negative to the positive. The group will shift from saying which option they do not like to identifying the one they prefer. Here it is helpful to explore the way in which one would put the selected option into operation. Will it work? Under what conditions? What problems might there be? Can a single religion ever be achieved? Can a system of "separate but equal" ever work? Some differences between that time and our time ought to be kept in mind. For instance, the Israelites did not conceive of a separation between "church and state." All cultures in the

Ancient Near East functioned as "theocracies." In the most general terms this meant that the political leader was also in some way the head of the religion.

There are other ways by which the group might evaluate the options. Sometimes a debate is a beneficial way to bring out the "pros" and "cons" of the different positions presented. The leader and the group should choose a way that most fits their style.

C. From Omri to Us. We also struggle with division in the various communities in which we participate. As the group is listing the options available to Omri and Ahab and evaluating those options, it is likely that individuals will relate the case to current situations. Statements arise like: "It is just like the split in the church." Or "It works the same way in a dispute between parents and children." Such statements connect with the present. They involve two current communities where divisions occur. The group might want to follow these up. There are many more.

Families must often handle divisions which are very deep. Each individual has her or his own identity which will come into conflict with the identity of another family member or members. Conflict can erupt over the question of how to spend discretionary time: vacations, evenings, weekends. Such a division was mentioned earlier in the Introduction. Deep divisions can arise over career conflicts. A situation in which both wife and husband have a career, a separate but equal situation, may run smoothly for some time. However, if one of them receives a transfer notice, the arrangement may break down. Then serious questions arise. What is the basis of the unity of the family? Should one push for family unity based on a single career? Admittedly this is a very complex matter and cannot be answered simplistically. However, working with the issue of unity and the way to achieve it in a community can provide an entré into family dilemmas.

One can move beyond the family to observe different

communities struggling with the issue of unity. Congregations can be divided over countless things. "Speaking in tongues" and "faith healing" are two examples which have been the focus of division. Congregations may be split over a new prayer book, hymnal, or confession of faith. These points of conflict also arise from fundamental differences: differences in doctrine, ritual, or behavior patterns. A split over the matter of faith healing is often founded on a basic difference in understanding of the way God works in the world. One faction understands God as intervening in the world to directly heal certain individuals under specific conditions. The other faction perceives God's healing as coming through the natural processes of human existence, through physicians and the human body's regenerative capacities. Healing is assumed to be available to all people. Such a difference in theology can create a fundamental split in the community. In such a situation the leadership of the congregation faces the same questions as Omri. What is the basis of unity? How do we establish unity?

Are the options which the group listed for Omri helpful in understanding ways to handle polarization in other communities? Groups often take the option of separation as the way to solve disunity in a community. Congregations divide into charismatics and noncharismatics. Spouses decide to obtain a divorce. Teen-agers opt to run away or parents put them out. In Omri's case, such a path would have meant two nations: one Canaanite, one Israelite. What are the alternatives to separation in situations of fundamental disunity, in families, congregations, nations? Remember, we are not considering moments of ruptured communication, but situations in which the division is deep and fundamental, like one nation with two gods.

D. *Summary.* A class discussion might move in this direction:
1. What are the options available to Omri and Ahab?
2. How would you evaluate the options? Which would you eliminate/prefer?

3. Where have you observed such fundamental disunity in families, congregations, nations, cities, schools? What alternatives are available to the leadership? Which alternative appears to you least/most beneficial?

The flow of a case discussion cannot be tightly programmed. This proposed direction may or may not "fit" well in a given setting.

Concerns to Consider

There are several issues which could be the focus of the discussion. Certainly the search for unity is a clear issue which arises in this case. The means of getting from a situation of disunity to one of unity is a companion concern. The next paragraphs will speak to these two issues with no pretention that they are the only issues which might be discussed or that they are being exhaustively explored here.

The Israelites and the Canaanites had things in common. They lived in the same geographical area. They were economically related to one another. The two groups had intermarried. All of this could form a basis for unity. However, they had two different religious "stories." We can obtain a feel for the difference this made by reading the literature of the two groups. The difference between the Baalism of the Canaanites and the Yahwism of the Israelites was so fundamental that no other basis of unity seemed to be sufficient.

We might ask about the basis for unity in the groups in which we participate. What is the basis of unity in the family? The family unit is initially established by a couple on the basis of courtship love and sealed by a public proclamation of commitment. This unity may be carried further by the birth or adoption of children. There are other things which strengthen the family unit. The most important element is that the family comes to have a common "life story": shared experiences, common values, etc.

However, as we know, all of this may not be enough. There

are also things which work against unity. The individuals in a family have their own life story: individual experiences which create distinctive personal values. These values will often clash with the values of other family members or the family as a whole. The problem then arises as it did in Israel. What is the basis of unity?

In Israel, religion was fundamental to unity. What about the family? In Christian tradition "love" has been understood to be the basis for family unity. If this is accepted, we must press on to say something about the character of love. What is love according to the biblical and theological tradition? Why is it a sufficient basis for unity?

All groups in which we participate struggle to discover a basis for unity that is sufficient to hold the community together. What is the basis for the union of the United States? Is it common land, religion, race? Is it acceptance of a certain governmental pattern (democracy), an economic system (capitalism), a view of humanity (worth of the individual)? Perhaps there is no one thing that holds the country together in terms of a single value or ideal. Perhaps unity grows out of a stream of experiences—a common story—which have shaped our values and brought us to this moment.

A church, both as a denomination and as a congregation, also works at this question. What forms the basis of unity in a church? For some it may be a set of beliefs, a creed, an affirmation of faith. For others unity may be focused in a style of worship: mass, revival meetings, healing services. Still other churches are held together by behavioral norms, such as personal morality, social service, and social action. Likely many of these play a part in varying degrees depending on the life story of the congregation or denomination. How would you describe the basis for unity in your church? Is it currently adequate?

Take a look at what it is that is fundamental to the unity of the groups in which you participate. You may want to push beyond those mentioned here to include others like service clubs, businesses, etc. What is it that holds the city together?

A companion concern involves the ways in which a group can move beyond disunity to unity. What do we do if there is no adequate basis for unity? This can happen to any group. In the case under discussion, division over religion prevented a solid unit from forming. Can division be overcome and a unit be (re-)established?

Certainly all the options which were available to Israel are still considered. Forced conformity, extermination, compromise, and separation are among the methods which groups use to try to overcome disunity. As we evaluate various methods, we would seldom consider extermination of one side as an acceptable method of solving a problem. However, war is predicated on the assumption that extermination is an effective and acceptable way of dealing with global disunity. This approach is also supported by television "police" shows and "western" movies.

Compromise is the method to which we most easily turn. Politics is often called the art of compromise. This is the option which Solomon suggested for Israel. When is that approach *not* appropriate?

Our understanding of appropriate leadership flows from the previous discussion. If we believe that compromise is the most beneficial approach, then we will look for a leader who will facilitate that. If we decide that forced conformity or extermination is the way to proceed, then we will look for a woman or man who can accomplish that. In a congregation, those who want unity based on "correct" doctrine will push for a pastor whose beliefs agree with theirs. Those who emphasize a set of behavioral standards as the foundation of a Christian community will want a leader who embodies those standards.

For these reasons a great deal of energy is spent in leadership selection. If is often assumed that the basis for unity and the method for obtaining unity is determined by the leader. To what extent is this assumption correct? Certainly David, Solomon, Omri, and Ahab had an important role in determining how Israel would resolve the religious question. The writer of Kings makes these leaders almost entirely responsible. Is that the way it works? Can a king, however strong, take a country on a path of his choice regardless of the will of the people? Can a president? Can a parent force a family into a certain mold? For how long? Some suggest that eventually people always have ways of working their will. This is true be it a child with a domineering parent, a congregation—whether the church polity be episcopal or congregational, a nation—whether their government be democratic or dictatorial. How important is leadership in helping determine the basis for corporate unity and the means to overcome division?

Resources to Read

II Samuel 8:1-18; I Kings 18:17-40

David incorporated a large number of diverse people into his kingdom. He established a centralized monarchy, which was new for Israel, in order to handle the problems of ruling a heterogeneous group. Elijah saw the diversity of religious beliefs as fundamentally problematic. The contest on Mt. Carmel sought to end the pluralism.

Anderson, Bernard W. *Understanding the Old Testament.* 3d. ed. Englewood Cliffs, New Jersey: Prentice-Hall, 1975. Pp. 139-47.

In Canaan it was understood that the fertility of the land was dependent upon Baal. Many people believed that the agricultural harvest was doomed if Baal was forgotten. For them Yahweh was the God of deliverance from strife, while Baal was the god of the fields.

Donner, Herbert. "The Separate States of Israel and Judah" in *Israelites and Judean History.* J. H. Hayes and J. M. Miller, eds. Philadelphia: Westminster Press, 1977. Pp. 399-414.

Samaria was planned from its beginning to be a capital from which Omri and his successors would rule according to the Canaanite model. Jezreel, the second capital in the northern state of Israel, would govern the Israelite population. Jehu clearly attempted to end the conflict between the Canaanites and Israelites by exterminating the Canaanites.

Fohrer, Georg. *History of the Israelite Religion.* D. E. Green, tr. Nashville: Abingdon, 1972. Pp. 230-31.

Ahab was trying to deal with the split between the Israelites and the Canaanites by treating both groups equally. Elijah objected to this approach. He declared that Yahweh alone was sovereign over the people. Yahweh and not Baal bestowed the rain and the crops and assured the fertility of the fields.

2.

The King and the Prophet

Introduction

This case is centered in the interaction between a king and a prophet. The interaction between kings and prophets in Israel was always unpredictable. This was due in part to the distinctive role of prophecy in Israel. It is difficult to say precisely who a prophet was and exactly what such a person did. It is somewhat easier to talk about a priest's role in the sanctuary, a sage teaching in school, or a king governing in Jerusalem. These leaders had defined social roles, but the same was not the case for the prophet.

This is evident when we look at the various ways a prophet could relate to a king. Sometimes the prophet would play the role of "king-maker." Saul, David, Solomon, and Jereboam I were among those monarchs who became king partly as a result of being anointed by a prophet. Besides being a king-maker, the prophet sometimes had a role as advisor to the king. The prophet might be part of the royal cabinet as Nathan was for David. But more often the king would go to the temple or a sanctuary to obtain counsel from a prophet. In God's sanctuary, the prophet would obtain a word or an "oracle" from God for the king. Still other prophets did not have a role in the royal court or any specific sanctuary. They might almost be called "free-lance" prophets. They had no attachment to any institution, but simply announced to the king or the people whatever message they received.

For these reasons a prophet's influence was unpredictable. His influence came less from any office which he might hold than from the persuasiveness of the message which he announced. For that reason, we call a prophet a charismatic rather than an institutional leader. Today we also experience people whose influence comes not from any office which they hold, but from the message which they bring. The message may be constructive or destructive, so we might include such diverse people as Martin Luther King, Che Guevara, Ralph Nader, and Billy Graham. The thing that these people have in common is that their influence came because of what they said and/or did and not because of any "office" they held or institutional position they occupied.

By contrast, the influence of a king came precisely because of the office he held. He was an institutional leader. The kings of Israel and Judah were installed by God and invested with given governmental responsibilities. They were installed into office as the anointed sons of God. "Messiah" is the Hebrew word for such persons. Furthermore, in Jerusalem the king was not just an individual installed by God, but a descendant of the house of David. The king always had to be a descendant of David.

We do not have the same experience with kings that Israel and Judah had. However, we do know about institutional leaders. We know people whose influence on our lives comes from the office they hold. One might think of people such as Jimmy Carter, Pope John Paul II, Kurt Waldheim, and Leonid Brezhnev. Again we might judge their influence constructive or destructive, but their authority and power still hold sway because of their institutional positions.

Isaiah was a charismatic leader with a message. Ahaz was an institutional leader with a responsibility. When the two met, the situation was ripe with possibilities and riddled with problems.[1]

The Case Study

Behold a young woman shall conceive and bear a son and shall call his name Immanuel. He shall eat curds and honey when he knows how to refuse the evil and choose the good. But before the boy knows how to refuse the evil and choose the good, the land before whose two kings you are in dread will be deserted. (Isa. 7:14b-16)

In 734 B.C., this word came from Isaiah to Ahaz, the king of Judah. It was directed to a specific political situation. Judah was threatened with military defeat by a coalition of armed forces from its northern neighbors, Israel and Syria. Isaiah's prophesy forbid Ahaz to take any military action against this invasion. It called on him to *be quiet* and *watch God act,* because before the boy Immanuel matured, God would destroy the invaders and devastate their land.

However, it was not clear that this was a wise course for Ahaz to follow. The invading army seemed able to move with ease against the army of Ahaz. Furthermore, Ahaz knew the goal of the Syria-Israel coalition. Their rulers wanted Ahaz off the throne. They wished to replace Ahaz with a person of their own choosing and not one from the "house of David." Ahaz could not allow this to happen. It was not just saving himself that was at stake. It was also a matter of preserving the "house of David." Tradition had preserved God's promise to David that one of his descendants would always sit on the throne in Jerusalem:

When your years are complete and you rest with your fathers, I will raise up your descendants after you, who shall come forth from your body, and I will establish his kingdom. He shall build a house for my name, and I will establish the throne of his kingdom forever. (II Sam. 7:12-13)

Could Ahaz afford to risk leaving his people, his throne, and himself defenseless by following Isaiah's advice? He had other options.

The Buffer States

The small states along the east coast of the Mediterranean Sea (see map below) had a long history of struggle between two powerful neighbors, Egypt to the South, and Assyria to the North. As "buffer states" they often found themselves unable to do anything except "obey the orders" of the more powerful nations. Nevertheless, they had always struggled to maintain some degree of independence. They had succeeded about a hundred years earlier by forming a coalition army. On that occasion their coalition had thwarted Assyria's attempt to intensify its control over them. However, Assyria was again seeking to dominate the area. The northern part of Syria had already fallen to Assyria as had the seacoast all the way down to Egypt.

So in 735 B.C., the Syrian states tried to form another coalition to stop Assyria. First Syria pressured Israel to join in battle against Assyria. These two states then demanded that Judah also join the coalition army against Assyria. Jotham was the King of Judah when the conspiracy against Assyria first developed. He refused to join. Very soon after he made that decision, Jotham died and the matter fell in the hands of his son, Ahaz. Ahaz tried to follow his father's decision, but he was unable to stop the invasion by his northern neighbors. Much of the Judaean countryside had already fallen to them. Besides this invasion by Syria and Israel, the Edomites were rebelling against Judah in the southeastern part of the land. Ahaz could not quell this rebellion either.

Assyrian Empire (or Ancient Near East)
735 B.C.

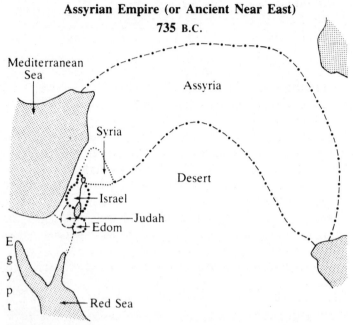

Options and Advice

Isaiah directed Ahaz to take no military action against this invasion from the North. God would intervene as Yahweh had before. God would come as a mighty warrior as Yahweh had at Israel's Exodus from Egypt: "Sing to Yahweh, for he has triumphed gloriously; the horse and his rider he has thrown into the sea" (Exod. 15:21).

God had indeed intervened in the past, but since then God had put a king on the throne. This was a new day. Ahaz was the anointed of Yahweh, the son of God.

> Why do the nations conspire,
>   and the people plot in vain?
> The kings of the earth set themselves,
>   and the rulers take counsel together,
>   against the Lord and his anointed. . . .

"I have set my king on Zion, my holy hill."
I will tell of the decreed of the Lord:
He said to me,
"You are my son,
    Today I have begotten you." (Ps. 2:1-2, 6-7)

Unlike before, God was governing Israel through a king. Could one really expect God to act now as he had at the Exodus? The times were different.

Ahaz had another option, one that would preserve his throne and maintain the existence of the people. He could call Assyria to Judah's rescue. Assyria's current military might was clearly visible. The Assyrian king, Tiglath-Pileser III, had recently conquered the Syrian city of Hamath. He had marched down the Mediterranean coast to establish an Assyrian outpost on the Egyptian border. Assyria could surely save Ahaz before Syria and Israel conquered him.

However, calling in Assyria was not without problems. To do so meant to pledge subservience to Assyria and its national gods. This would involve paying heavy taxes to Assyria. It might necessitate building an Assyrian temple in Jerusalem. It was a price that Isaiah considered too great. This would be a serious compromise of the first commandment: "You shall have no other gods before me" (Exod. 20).

Ahaz, the anointed of God, faced the problem of preserving Judah. He also faced the problem of preserving the throne of David in a way that none of his davidic predecessors had faced. Assyria would help, but for a price. The prophet Isaiah demanded that Ahaz risk losing all and depend on the intervention of God to deliver the people.

Communiqué to Learners and Teachers

Directions for Discussion

Groups who discuss this case differ. They differ in the extent to which they know the event which this case lifts up.

They differ in the degree to which they enjoy involving themselves in activities such as role playing. The one who is directing the discussion will need to choose a path which he or she thinks is a good match between the case and the class.

A. Identifying the options. It is often helpful to begin the discussion by identifying the options which Ahaz has. This helps the group sort the case out and establish the particulars of the case so that they are clear to all participants. The options which are usually identified include:

1. Doing nothing about the threat from Syria and Israel.
2. Joining Syria and Israel against Assyria.
3. Calling on Assyria for help against Syria and Israel.

Many times there is benefit in going beyond these three options and allowing a free flow of ideas about options not made explicit in the case. We can learn from suggestions which sound like nonsense. Some suggestions which have been made such as "call in the U.S. Air Force" or "surrender to Israel and Syria and engage in guerilla warfare," may seem silly. But we need to take a second look at such answers. In the first place, they point up the differences between our time and theirs. Secondly, they push us to evaluate our own situation. In what way does the U.S. act like Assyria, willing to intervene, but for a price? To keep from being crushed in a "head to head" confrontation, guerilla warfare and sabotage are weapons used by a weaker party to avoid compromising with a stronger party.

B. Evaluating the king's decision. It may be that the group does not know what action the king did take. In that case the discussion leader might proceed by asking, "Of all the options presented, which option do you prefer?" It is important to examine the reasons for such a decision. Sometimes it is fun to set up a debate between Isaiah and Ahaz.

On the other hand, many groups already know that Ahaz decided to call in Assyria. They also know that the Bible judges his decision unfaithful. If such is the case, it might be best not to play the game "Let's pretend that we don't know." It might be better to begin at a different place. Why did Ahaz choose to call in Assyria? What do you think about that decision? Do you feel absolute condemnation of his decision is justified?

As mentioned in the introduction, the prophet is a charismatic type of leader in that the authority depends on the persuasiveness of the prophet's message and person. The king is an institutional leader in that his authority comes by virtue of the office he occupies. Why should the king, anointed by God to rule, listen to a prophet? Who are the "prophets" and "kings" in our day? Where do you see clashes between charismatic leaders and institutional leaders? With which views do you identify?

C. Choosing when to risk. In this case the prophet might be called "idealistic." He told the institutional leader to stand quietly and wait for Yahweh's deliverance. Isaiah called on Ahaz to risk losing everything at this moment in Judah's history. The king made a pragmatic decision. He took a direction which he thought had the best chance of insuring survival. Ahaz apparently decided that it was wiser to give homage to Assyrian gods than to risk immediate death and destruction.

Perhaps no issue is more difficult in this case than the question of risk. When is the time to risk? Is it ever right to "play it safe" as Ahaz did?

Jesus did not play it safe. He made a decision to "set his face to go to Jerusalem." Jesus decided to risk losing all that he had lived and worked for by going the "way of the cross." On the other hand, Acts 9:23-25 narrates that Paul decided that there was a time to "play it safe." When faced with the plot of some Jews to kill him in Damascus, Paul escaped over the wall in a basket.

When is it appropriate to play it safe? When are we called on to go the "way of the cross"? Can we ever know for sure which time is which?

D. *Summary.* A discussion of this case might move as follows:
1. What are the options which Ahaz has?
2. Which option do you prefer? Or how do you evaluate Ahaz' decision to call in Assyria?
3. When is it time to "play it safe"; when is it time to risk losing everything?

Concerns to Consider

As we become involved in this case, let us identify some of the issues which are raised by it. A case seldom has only one issue. Certainly that is true with **The King and the Prophet.** The question of compromise is one of the issues at stake here. Another is the conflict between a charismatic type of leader and an institutionally designated leader. There are certainly more issues which will arise in the course of a group discussion of this case. Let us look for a moment at the two issues mentioned above.

A. *The question of compromise.* There are few among us who consider themselves "purists," that is, ones who condemn compromise under any circumstance. In our minds compromise is often associated with politics. However, those of us who are not in "politics" as such still understand what it means to compromise. The program of a church is usually the result of compromise. Some people wish the church to have an active social witness. Others see spiritual growth as the primary need. Still others want a strong evangelistic program to be the chief goal. The program which is actualized is usually a compromise of some sort.

While all of us compromise at many points in our lives, we are often uneasy about it. We are not sure where and when compromise is acceptable. Indeed, we are not sure that compromise is ever the "will of God." This study does not raise the question of compromise in general, but in terms of this specific situation.

In this moment from Israel's history, Isaiah considered a compromise to be wrong. Isaiah said that in this situation compromise was not the will of God. He directed the king to risk letting Judah be defeated rather than compromise. Isaiah asserted that God would intervene to deliver the people from trouble as Yahweh had in the time of the Exodus from Egypt. As they did in the face of Pharaoh's army, the people were to stand quietly and observe God's act of salvation.

The alternative, compromise, was intolerable to Isaiah. To submit to Assyria and to that nation's gods would be to turn their back on Israel's God. It would mean violating the first commandment: "You shall have no other gods before me."

But was it that simple? Was this the moment to risk losing everything? Or was it not more prudent for Ahaz to call in Assyria, to compromise, so that the throne and the land could be preserved?

If we look closely, we see that a matter of "power" complicates this situation. It is not hard to see what Ahaz was up against just by looking at the map on page 106. Assyria dwarfed the small buffer states. The Assyrian general/king, Tiglath-Pileser III, was aiming to extend his power to the border of Egypt. That meant trouble for the smaller states in his path. It set up the dilemma which Ahaz faced. Ahaz had very little power to stand up against either Assyria or the Syria-Israelite coalition. Would it be anything less than suicidal for Ahaz not to compromise? Wouldn't he have had to pledge subservience to Assyria sooner or later?

We meet questions of compromise every day, moments when it seems prudent to compromise even our most firmly held convictions. In a high school history class, a young man encountered one of those moments. The teacher had a very clear position on the American Revolution. He asserted that war was the only way that the colonies could have obtained their freedom. As supplementary reading, Ed had read an article that challenged the teacher's position. According to this article, England was not in a position to carry through the repressive measures much longer. As a child growing up in a family opposed to war, Ed had been taught that there were alternatives to war. War was the wrong way to go. Love, even if it meant sacrificing one's own life, was the only way to break the circle of violence. War brings more hatred and more killing. Ed raised this possibility in class. The teacher labeled such a position "absurd." Soon the time came for the final test. Ed looked at the essay question: "Was the American Revolution necessary? Support your answer with facts." He did not know what to do. If Ed wrote what he believed, he was sure what the result would be and good grades were important to get into college. This was a moment in which compromise was complicated by power. Integrity insisted that Ed not compromise, but the teacher had all the power. What experience have you had in which you felt forced to compromise for the sake of survival? This was the situation of Ahaz. Can such compromise be considered the God-ordained way? Or does it always fall short of what we know is expected of us?

B. The quesion of leadership. A second major issue in this case is the conflict between a charismatic type of leader and an institutionally designated one. Isaiah was the charismatic figure. He had no institutional authority. His only power was the persuasiveness of his person and his message. Did Isaiah proclaim the true word from God?

Ahaz was the institutional figure. He had an office and that office gave him authority. His authority was not only human political power. He was anointed by God to this office. He too had a right to speak and act for God.

What happens when there is a clash between two such figures: the charismatic leader and the institutional leader?

We have experienced such clashes. We are familiar with the

clash between Martin Luther King, Jr. and George Wallace over integration, and the clash between Ralph Nader and General Motors over auto safety. Similar dynamics are also present in other situations in which we ourselves may have been directly involved. A young couple stood against the use of radiation and chemicals in the treatment of their child's cancer: "We want our child to live or die with dignity. We think radiation and chemicals are wrong. Good food and God are the best chance for our child." The hospital had to decide whether to take the matter to court. Who is speaking the true word: the couple who has no sanctioned medical authority or the institution which is given authority in medical matters?

A young woman announced to her parents that she was "living with" her boyfriend because "marriage as it is currently being practiced is nothing more than legalized slavery. The church by supporting marriage is supporting the enslavement of women." A priest began to ordain persons on his own because the reforms of the Vatican were "leading the church away from the *true* faith." All of these scenes share one thing in common: they represent a clash between a person who claims to have the truth against an institution and its leadership who assert that they "know best."

Who has the "true" word from God? Is it the charismatic type of leader like Isaiah? Is it the institutional leader like Ahaz? Making a decision is not easy, but it is a decision we all face.

Resources to Read

II Kings 16:1-20; Isaiah 7:1-17; II Chronicles 28:1-27

Both the authors of II Kings and II Chronicles wrote with the assumption that Ahaz made an unfaithful decision. II Chronicles even elaborated the narrative to emphasize the unfaithfulness of Ahaz. Isaiah 7 was written from the prophetic point of view. How might a narrative from the king's perspective be written?

Fohrer, Georg. *History of Israelite Religion.* Nashville: Abingdon, 1972. Pp. 139-50, 235-43.

Fohrer describes what it meant for the king to be called the "son" of God. He describes the prophets as "messengers of God." Through his discussion and bibliography we can learn more about the king as an institutional leader and the prophet as a charismatic leader.

MacLean, H. B. "Ahaz" in *The Interpreter's Dictionary of the Bible.* Vol. A–D. Nashville: Abingdon Press, 1962. Pp. 64-66.

Maclean notes that Ahaz was only twenty years old when he was thrust into this situation by his father's death. The author also portrays some of the "cost" of earning survival by alliance with Assyria.

Kaiser, Otto. *Isaiah 1–12.* Philadelphia: Westminster Press, 1972. Pp. 87-106.

In his discussion of Israel's history, Kaiser states the issue from Isaiah's point of view. Do leaders have power to void the promises of God to protect the people, or does God have the power to void the evil plans of people?

Notes

1. Among the discussions of prophecy and kingship which might be read for more detail are Walther Zimmerli, *Old Testament Theology in Outline* (Atlanta: John Knox Press, 1978), pp. 81-108; Gerhard von Rad, *The Message of the Prophets* (New York: Harper & Row, 1967), pp. 15-78; Walther Eichrodt, *Theology of the Old Testament,* Vol. I (Philadelphia: Westminster Press, 1961), pp. 289-344, 436-51.

3.
The Conscience and the Community

Introduction

Each of us has experienced that inner agent of knowing which we call the conscience. Although at one time it was assumed that the conscience was an inner sense of absolute truth, we now observe that everyone's conscience sends him or her different messages. The messages we receive from the conscience are affected by the roads we travel in our life pilgrimage. This does not mean, however, that the information from the conscience is less valuable. It means only that the information is of a different kind than we had thought at one time.

The information we receive from the conscience is relational information. It guides us in our relationships with other people. It is probably less correct to say that the conscience tells us right from wrong, than to say that it tells us what is helpful and harmful to our relationships. For example, a child is guided by his or her conscience not to eat a piece of candy just before the evening meal. The conscience is not telling the child that the candy is bad or even that it is wrong to eat candy before a meal. More accurately, the conscience is saying that it will be harmful to your relationship with your parents if you eat that candy now. That is important information to have.

It is the same with adults. Jean received messages from her conscience. In response, she decided to participate in an act of civil disobedience aimed at calling attention to the manufacture of nuclear weapons at Rocky Flats, Colorado. While participating in a sit-in, she wrote a Mother's Day prayer explaining her reasons for protesting.

God, who is power and truth, I'm on these railroad tracks into Rocky Flats on Mother's Day 1978 because 8 years ago and 3 years ago I gave birth to two baby girls. Today I am here praying for their continued life and health on this planet.

The prayer goes on, showing that Jean's conscience gave her information about her responsibility not only to her own children, but to all children. Information about our responsibility in relationship to other people is important information for us to have.

There are times when we are unclear about our relationship to others. Then we are not sure what our responsibility is. At such times the conscience may send mixed or confused messages. This can happen with a newly married couple. It is often the problem between college roommates or singles who share an apartment. In such a situation one may act in ways that are harmful to the relationship without any inner sense that such will be the case. The conscience is not sufficiently informed about the relationship to know what is beneficial or detrimental.

The Corinthian Church was a community of new Christians. They were learning what it meant to be a part of a new body. How were they to behave toward one another? What was the relationship of Christianity to their previous religious communities? It was to be expected that the consciences of individual members would give different messages and therefore understand new behaviors in disparate ways. A problem arose over the meat which was eaten at the community meal, meat that had been "sacrificed" to idols.

The Case Study

There are some, being accustomed to idols up until now, who eat food as if it were sacrificed to an idol; and their conscience, being weak, is defiled. (I Cor. 8:7b)

Most of the meat which was available in markets of Corinth had come from a sacrificial ritual. In a formal temple ritual food was set before the altar of a god or goddess. In that way it was being "sacrificed" to the idol. This made the meat "holy," according to various religions of the Roman Empire.

The gospel, as interpreted by Paul, laughed at such nonsense. The idols were not real. Setting meat on a table in front of a statue did not change the character of the food. The meat was exactly the same as it had been before the "ritual." A Christian was free to eat any meat he or she chose: "What God has cleansed, cannot be considered profane" (Acts 10:15b).

This worked smoothly for many in the community. They were now free from the confines of clean and unclean meat inherited from the Jewish tradition. They were also released from the bondage of considering food profane because it had been set on the altar of some other religion. The Christian was free to eat anything.

However, the new ways were not easily assimilated by everyone. There were some whose previous experience of eating this food was still very much inside them. They were not able to break the connection between the food and the holy place where it had been "sacrificed." Their conscience was still guided by the previous religious group with which they had been associated. Their conscience was not yet strongly connected with their new community, the body of Christ.

As the church at Corinth sat down to eat together, most of the Christians could enjoy the food as part of God's good creation. Those who as yet had a "weak conscience" enjoyed the meal too, but as they ate something happened to them which was not helpful. For them the conscience was still taking its cues from their previous religious group, it sent them the wrong messages. The conscience said, "You are eating holy meat. By eating this 'sacred' food, Christians are connected with members of other religions as *one people*."

The message which Paul had brought to Corinth was not that at all. Paul was calling people to a new community, a group distinctly set apart, the body of Christ. Those members with a "strong" conscience, one firmly rooted in the new community, would understand why they could eat the meat. When those with a "weak" conscience ate the food, however, their understanding of the Christian faith became muddled, and they stumbled.

Paul had several options. He could exhort those of weaker conscience to become more firmly rooted in the body of Christ: "Be strong in the faith." He might encourage those who were strong to model clear thinking, that is, the ability to keep the present separate from the old ritual experiences surrounding meat. He might have permitted the strong to give free expression to their faith without being shackled by the weakness of a few. Paul's direct advice was different:

Be careful lest this freedom of yours become a pitfall for those who are weak. . . . For through your knowledge, one who is weak, a brother for whom Christ died, may be ruined. . . . Therefore, if food might be the reason for my brother's downfall, I will never eat meat again, in order that I not cause my brother's downfall. (I Cor. 8:9, 11, 13)

Communiqué for Learners and Teachers

Directions for Discussion

This case centers on a problem in the Corinthian Church. The meals which the community had been eating together were being understood differently by different participants. One avenue of discussion would be to explore whether and where we should curtail our freedom in order not to cause "weaker" persons to stumble. While not ignoring this possibility, the suggestions that follow will lead in a different direction. It is hoped that through discussion we can better understand what Paul meant by conscience and the difference between a "weak" conscience and a "strong" one. Then perhaps we will know what it means to choose not to "eat meat" in order that "I not cause my brother's downfall" in our own lives.

A. Exploring Paul's advice. The group might start out by taking a poll. How many agree with Paul's advice? Then the group might talk together about the reasons for the vote they cast. Such a discussion can be organized by listing the advantages and disadvantages of the advice that Paul gave. The following is a sample list which other groups have offered.

Advantages:

1. Paul's advice puts the burden for action on the group best able to handle it, the strong.
2. By acting on Paul's advice, the strong become an example of a willingness to limit oneself for the sake of others.
3. Eating the meat was not essential.
4. The "weak" are accepted as they are and not forced to change.

Disadvantages:

1. It lets the "weak" remain weak; they are not challenged to grow.
2. It permits the behavior of the whole group to be determined by its weakest member.
3. It inhibits the maturation of the group by ceasing an activity rather than really working at the causes of the problem.

Each group will have other things to add to this sample list and other ways of expressing these ideas.

Having a list of the disadvantages as well as the advantages of the advice which Paul gave, the group might want to explore changes they would want to make or suggestions they would add to Paul's advice. One of the suggestions that has been frequently mentioned is that the church at Corinth cease eating "idol" meat for a while until the strong can "educate" the weak. The hope is that if the Corinthian church would sit down and study and talk with one another, the "weak" could be strengthened. Then the whole community could resume eating the meat and have a common understanding about it. How easily can such a change in perspective be brought about? Before we can answer that completely, it may be necessary to understand some of Paul's perception of "conscience."

B. Conscience and the community. Customarily we think of conscience as that inner sense of what is right and wrong, but we are aware that conscience is not something we had at birth. One's conscience sometimes guides in quite different directions from the conscience of another. A lot of different people in our lives have helped shape the conscience, the inner sense of what is the most appropriate behavior. Think for a bit about all of the different people and groups who have been instrumental in the development of your conscience. The discussion group might make a list of those:

1. Parents
2. Other family
3. Neighbors
4. Friends at church
5. Teachers
6. Peers at school or work
7. Newspapers, television

This is obviously a partial list and a general one. It may be more helpful to the group to make the list more specific.

Which family members, friends, teachers do you remember as especially significant in your developing a sense of "right and wrong"? What exactly did they contribute? Sometimes we cannot analyze exactly what each contributed, but we can often recall a story about the other person which will illustrate their contribution. How do you think our sense of appropriate and inappropriate behavior has been influenced by the mass media? Television is praised and blamed as being especially influential here. List the ways that the group thinks the media has aided the development of conscience in positive and negative ways. How do we understand God to be related to the development of conscience?

C. Conscience and the Christian community. Now perhaps we can look at the case in a new light. The person who had a "weak conscience" was one whose understanding was guided by a previous community; in this situation it was a previous religious community. This was causing the person to misinterpret the meal. Paul advises that the strong stop eating the meat rather than involve some of the community in something that they misunderstand. How can one strengthen the conscience of the "weak"? How can one enable the "weak" to make the shift so that his or her actions and attitudes are guided less by other communities and relationships and more by the body of Christ? Remember that conscience is not a matter of "thoughts" alone, but is that inner sense which guides our actions and attitudes. It was developed over a lifetime. Is such a shift sudden or gradual? How might the community facilitate a change?

One final thing the group might want to explore: for Paul, having one's conscience reformed in the Christian community was a freeing thing. Is this true for you or do you find the Christian conscience as you have experienced it restrictive? If it is restrictive, why is this? Has the church misunderstood the purpose of the conscience? Are there other factors involved?

D. Summary. A format for discussion of this case might procede as follows:

1. What arc the advantages and disadvantages of Paul's advice?
2. What changes or additions would you make to Paul's counsel?
3. What relationships in your life have helped shape your conscience?
4. How can we strengthen those people whose consciences are only weakly connected with the Christian community?

Concerns to Consider

There are a variety of issues which might be explored in this case. One might look at the value of Paul's intervention in a community dispute. On what grounds does a person have a right to intervene from the "outside," if in fact Paul could be considered an outsider? Another issue involves the distinctiveness of Christianity from other groups. Paul was interested in maintaining that Christians not understand themselves as united with the other religious groups of the Roman Empire. However, this "Communiqué" has centered its attention on the conscience, as understood by Paul, and on ways in which the conscience can be strengthened.

A. Punitive and guiding conscience. Most people have had the experience of the conscience as an internalized "No." It is an internal mechanism that condemns us when we transgress a boundary. Psychoanalytic theory maintains that this condemning conscience can be traced to the restrictions put on us when we were children. When restrictions were laid on us by our parents who were so much more powerful than we were, we had no choice except to obey. Gradually we internalized this "no" from our parents so that even when our parents were not around the "no" could still be heard in certain situations. That is simplified, but in essence that is how we all come to have a condemning conscience. Many argue that the condemning conscience is not a life-enhancing mechanism. They say it is a life-restricting agent. Can you recall an experience with your condemning conscience? Do you agree that it is restrictive rather than helpful to a person's life pilgrimage?

If it is agreed that a conscience which simply condemns a person when she or he has transgressed a childhood boundary is not helpful, there is a remaining question. Is there another function of the conscience which we can observe? Donald Miller works at this question in his book, *The Wing-Footed Wanderer: Conscience and Transcendence.* There he describes what is called a sponsoring or guiding conscience. This conscience does not necessarily say "no"; it also says "yes." It encourages people to forge ahead and act in ways that are beneficial to life. One of the classic stories of the sponsoring conscience is in Mark Twain's *Huckleberry Finn.* Huck had helped his slave friend Jim escape. The two of them were on the raft when men came hunting for Jim. Huck had to decide whether or not to turn Jim in. His condemning conscience was going to accuse him either way—for turning in a friend or for telling a lie. He decided to lie and created a story which made the slave hunters think that someone on the raft had smallpox. That was his guiding conscience. The sponsoring conscience encourages the individual toward life-affirming decisions.

The guiding or sponsoring conscience is much closer to the way in which Paul seems to be using the term, than is the condemning, accusing conscience. Like the latter, the sponsoring conscience develops from interaction with other people. Only in this case it is not traced to restrictions which a child had to obey. Rather, the sponsoring conscience develops over a whole lifetime of relationships with people, certainly beginning with parents and moving on from there. William Sloan Coffin, pastor of Riverside Church in New York, describes the development of his sponsoring conscience in his autobiography, *Once to Every Man.* He tells of his pilgrimage from being an officer in World War II through a period with the CIA, to joining the Civil Rights movement, and finally becoming a leader against the war in Vietnam. He tells this story of sharp contrasts not as a person driven by the guilt of a condemning conscience. His stance against the war in Vietnam does not cause him to look back on his time with the CIA in accusation. Rather various experiences with people enhanced within him the urge to move in new ways. These included civil disobedience in both the Civil Rights and the Anti-War movements. Others will condemn him, but his conscience guides him on in what he understands to be life-affirming ways.

Have you had experiences where your sponsoring conscience guided you to act? These actions may have broken through the restrictive barrier of your own condemning conscience or the condemnation of others. How can we facilitate in one another the development of a sponsoring conscience within the context of the Christian community? Often times we seem to reinforce the restrictive consciences in one another. A strong sponsoring conscience would allow us the freedom to take life-affirming actions.

B. Limiting our actions. Paul chose to limit his own actions so as to avoid being harmful to other persons. Some people question Paul's self-limiting action. This is partly due to the way this text has been interpreted. Many have proposed that Paul gave up eating meat to avoid enticing a person to eat "sacrificed" meat when it was against the person's "restrictive conscience." So interpreted, Paul would be allowing a person to remain a prisoner of his or her condemning conscience. One young man called Paul "gutless." This youth declared that Paul should stand up for what he believed and give the other person the chance to stand up for what that person believed. If the "weaker" person could not stand up for his or her beliefs, then maybe someone would be around to "pick up the pieces."

Whether or not we agree with the young man's assessment, this case suggests that we interpret Paul's situation differently. It was not a matter of enticing someone to eat the food. The Corinthian Church was already eating this food together. Persons with a weak conscience misunderstood the meal. They thought that they were eating a meal in communion with idol worshipers.

Paul was willing to give up eating the meat rather than have the meal misinterpreted by the participants. Can we find an analogy? Reference was made above to civil disobedience in both the Civil Rights and the Anti-War movements. Before Martin Luther King, Jr. led any march, he sought to make sure that the action was not misunderstood by any of the participants. Much time and effort was taken to try to insure that each marcher knew the motivation, the goal, and the methods of the march. Martin Luther King would call off a march if there were not time to obtain this necessary clarity. One has to say that clarity did not always happen, and when there was misunderstanding of the march on the part of the participants, problems often arose with their behavior. Of course outsiders could have a lot of different interpretations of the King marches and they did. So also the community meal of the church at Corinth was interpreted in a number of ways by outsiders. However, problems developed if the participants themselves misunderstood the meal.

Here is another example. The Rankin family consisted of Ed, Pat, and their children, Steve, 17, Jan, 14, and Cindy, 12. Cindy was to be in her first Junior High band concert and it was decided that the whole family would go. After the concert, but before Cindy joined them, they had an interesting difference of opinion about the concert. Ed and Jan though it was a waste of time: "The music was terrible." To this Steve responded, "We didn't go for the music. We went to be with Cindy." Two of the family members had misinterpreted the meaning of their presence at the concert, and they were miserable. Now obviously the family would not have called off going to the concert had they known misinterpretations would arise, but they might have altered the decision that the whole family would go.

Paul decided that it was better to stop eating the meal than to have it misinterpreted by some of the participants. Is there any time that we should go ahead even if not everyone is "on board"? Paul decided not to go on because those with a "weak conscience" would "stumble." Again, it was not a matter of the weak's being tempted to do something against their punitive conscience. Paul's concern was that because their conscience was not strongly informed by the Christian community they would misconstrue the whole Christian perspective. Is "being defiled" or "stumbling" an adequate guideline? How would you go about setting out the criteria in more detail?

Resources to Read

I Corinthians 8:1-13

Idols were representatives of gods that did not exist. There was no reason why the Corinthians could not eat food set at the table of nonexistent gods, except that it was causing problems in the community. Paul counseled the strong against letting their freedom be the instrument through which other community members ran into difficulty.

Conzelmann, Hans. *I Corinthians* (Hermeneia Series). Philadelphia: Fortress Press, 1975. Pp. 146-50.

Paul advised the strong to limit their freedom on behalf of the weak. He gave no advice either to the strong or the weak on how the weak could be strengthened. Paul allowed the weak to be as they were and did not push them to conform to an ideal standard.

Baird, William. *The Corinthian Church—A Biblical Approach to Urban Culture.* Nashville: Abingdon Press, 1964. Pp. 18-23.

The culture during New Testament times was quite different from our situation. Yet churches located in an urban setting had the same problems that plague us. This is especially true of the church at Corinth, which was located in a cosmopolitan center struggling with economic disparity between the rich and the poor.

Miller, Donald E. *The Wing-Footed Wanderer: Conscience and Transcendence.* Nashville: Abingdon, 1977.

The condemning conscience restricts a person's life, but the sponsoring conscience guides a person toward fullness of life. Psychologists are correct in seeing the condemning conscience as a problem to be dealt with. However, we must also describe the guiding function of the conscience. Life is lived between the inhibiting and guiding conscience.

4.

The Family
and the Kingdom of God

Introduction

One of the things that makes an individual's life complex is the different roles she or he is expected to play. Almost daily these roles collide and one has to decide which role will get the available time and energy. The crisis created by role conflict is not limited to any age group. Young children have it the easiest, but even for children there are rough moments. For example, language which is used with neighborhood play-mates may cause trouble when used at home. The clash of role responsibilities for the adolescent is often explosive: home, school, friends. There has been a great deal of discussion recently concerning role conflicts in adults, especially for women who are responsible to both a family and a career.

The problems created by the clash of responsibilities are severe for all men and women. The clash is no less problematic for the Christian; in fact it may even be more agonizing. This is often true when one understands him or herself "called by God" to a certain set of tasks, e.g. social service or pastoral ministry. One then ends up with one set of tasks which seems to have divine sanction and another set of responsibilities without that sanction, but nevertheless compelling, e.g.

career, family. Such a bind can result in anguish for the person, but also for those around him or her. For example, Jan was forced to pay the price for the bind her husband experienced between his call to the pastoral ministry and family responsibilities. Over and over again Jan heard comments like, "The picnic will have to wait. You know that my work at the church has to come first. I've been called by God to this work and I must be responsible to it." Jan never knew what to say.

It is not just in clergy families that such conflict arises. Sandy understood her work at the inner city youth center as just as legitimately a "calling" to God's work as any pastor. This volunteer work involved her every week day from 3:00 to 9:00 P.M. Sandy's husband and children were angry with that. It was mildly inconvenient at evening mealtime, but more aggravating was the fact that the children almost never had time with their mother.

The Family and the Kingdom of God looks at precisely this problem as it is reflected in specific texts from the Gospels. In particular, it centers in on the clash between responsibility to family as called for in the fifth commandment and affirmed in Mark 7:10-13 and responsibility to the work of the kingdom of God. Those two responsibilities do not always fit well together.

The Case Study

Moses said, "Honor your father and your mother," and "Anyone who speaks evil against father or mother shall be put to death." But you say, "If a person says to their father or mother, 'Anything that I might have used to help you is Corban (that is, given to God),' " thus you prevent them from doing anything for their father and mother. This makes the word of God null and void for the sake of tradition. (Mark 7:10-13)

For the Pharisee, obedience to God was considered even more important than love to father or mother. The Corban was one way in which this obedience to God was shown. According to this practice a person dedicated his or her estate to God. The person was free to use the "dedicated" goods to sustain his or her own life, but those goods could not be given to anyone else or used for any other purpose. Such a "will" was irrevocable so even if one's own parents needed the money, it could not be used for them. It now belonged to God and could only be used for God's kingdom. At the person's death, the whole estate went to the synagogue or temple.

For Jesus, human need took precedence over all other demands. Judged by this criterion the Corban was indefensible. When faced with the needs of their parents, the ones who had willed their estate to God could only say, "I am sorry. All that I have with which I might have helped you has been given to God." Not only did that run against the basic responsibility to the people in need, it violated the fifth commandment: "Honor your father and your mother that your days may be long in the land which Yahweh, your God gives you" (Exod. 20:12). The practice of Corban disregarded the fundamental requirement that a person respond to human need wherever it occurs and the commandment which required that one meet the needs of one's parents without qualification. According to this, one could not use obedience to God as a way around family responsibility.

For the disciples of Jesus, on the other hand, obedience to God was in fact to be more important than love of father and mother.

If anyone comes to me and does not hate his or her own father and mother and spouse and children and brothers and sisters, yes, even one's own life, such a person is not able to become my disciple. (Luke 14:26)

Anyone who loves father or mother more than me is not worthy of me. Anyone who loves a son or daughter more than me is not worthy of me. (Matt. 10:37)

The kingdom of God was understood to have first priority in the life of every person. There was no other allegiance which dared to share first place with the work of the "kingdom," not even allegiance to one's own family. A person had to be willing to lay aside everything to follow Jesus: "[Jesus] said to him, 'Let the dead bury their own dead; as for you, go and announce the kingdom of God' " (Luke 9:60). Obedience to God took precedence over the most basic human relationships and duties.

Two traditions stand side by side in the values Jesus was affirming. Each person was responsible to care for his family and no practice in the name of "obedience to God" could automatically annul that. However, the call to follow Jesus dared not be interrupted or delayed by duties to family. Both of these values were lifted up, even though the tradition knew they often clashed with each other.

Communiqué to Learners and Teachers

Directions for Discussion

In this case we are presented with two different traditions which stand side by side in the values Jesus affirmed. Both deal with family responsibility, but they come out at two different places. Because this case does not intend to focus on an event in the life of the early church or ancient Israel, the entré into this discussion will need to be a bit different than some of the other cases where an event calling for a decision is central. The following is given as one way a discussion of **The Family and the Kingdom of God** might move, but there may be other plans for discussion which would fit a particular group better. Discussion leaders are encouraged to develop their own plans.

A. *Responsibility as a family member.* The group can begin by formulating a list of family responsibilities. The list will vary, of course, depending on the individuals making the suggestions. Here is a very partial list as an example:

1. Talk to parents.
2. Earn money for family food, clothing, shelter.
3. Service the home.
4. Shop for food, clothing, and housing needs.
5. Teach children through games and activities.
6. Listen to and share with spouse.
7. Spend time with siblings.
8. Visit widowed aunt.

The list of family responsibilities can get quite extensive. It is often helpful to bring some order out of what might otherwise be a chaotic list by separating the family into groups and by listing the responsibilities which one has to each part of what we call family. The following list is one suggestion:

1. Spouse
2. Children
3. Parents
4. Siblings
5. Extended family

Under "extended family" one would include grandparents, aunts and uncles, cousins, etc. Obviously the categories that are used will depend on the age of the discussants, and in no way should it be assumed that "family" refers to spouse and children. Each group member will define her or his family a little differently. For a single adult, siblings and parents may be the most significant family, or perhaps even nieces and nephews. The most important thing is not to shut people out of the discussion by the way "family" is defined.

Notice from the list the amount of time that is invested in meeting family needs. There is the time spent in earning money to meet physical needs. It takes time to shop for groceries and clothes and to care for property and automobiles. Then of course there is time spent visiting family members in response to their social and emotional needs. Some families are even willing to invest time in sharing ideas and stimulating one another's thinking. The list will reveal many other ways in which family responsibility calls for an investment of time and energy. What percentage of our time goes into meeting family needs?

B. Responsibility as a Christian. According to most Christian groups, an individual becomes a Christian by adult baptism or by confirmation in the faith as an adult. At that time a person takes on another set of responsibilities. This is usually indicated by a baptismal or confirmation statement in which one agrees to support the work of Christ with her or his resources: time, money, talents, energy, etc. This means that individuals have their own "ministerial" responsibilities as persons who have dedicated their lives to the kingdom of God. Some people give enormous amounts of their time to carrying out their ministry. Others have guilt feelings when they think of what they promised to do as a Christian as compared with their actual performance. There are many reasons for the difference between promise and performance, but by all odds the most frequently voiced reason is that we do not have the time or energy to do the things we know we should.

It may be beneficial for the discussion group to make a second list. This list will include the responsibilities which one has as a Christian. It would be appropriate to include caring for personal family needs as one of the responsibilities of a Christian, but let us set that one aside for a moment. Instead think of the responsibilities which one has as a member of the "body of Christ," the Christian family. This list should of course include those things which the individual is already doing. But it should also include those things which we feel we could and/or should be doing had we the time and energy. Included in this list could be a wide variety of tasks such as:

1. Volunteering for work at the hospital.
2. Teaching in the church school.
3. Taking lay training classes in religion.
4. Participating in a prison visitation program.
5. Setting aside time for daily prayer.
6. Studying for the pastoral ministry.
7. Running for the school board.

Again it is often beneficial if one organizes the various responses. The terms chosen to organize the responses should reflect the character of the group and the terms with which that group is familiar. Responses have sometimes been grouped together under categories such as these: education, nurture, counseling, evangelism, proclamation, witness, service, relief work, social action. Certainly these are not all the possible categories, but if the discussion leader has thought of a range of categories ahead of time, then he or she can help organize the responses that come up. Obviously the categories have to be flexible and the group may wish to add different ones. It is also important to listen carefully when a person describes what he or she is or would like to be doing. Some individuals understand their music as witness and evangelism. Others understand their music more in terms of teaching or nurture.

This list too will be quite lengthy especially as the group adds the things that they really should or would like to be doing. For example, a person will often say that she or he would really like to visit in the neighborhood, among church members, or at the hospital if the time and energy were just available. Another may long for the opportunity to work with troubled youngsters or marriage enrichment seminars if there were only enough time. Still another may say that he or she would like to take his or her agricultural, industrial, or crafts skills to assist people in another country, if it were not for home responsibilities. All of these may be a part of one's ministry as Christians. Do these responsibilities have a higher claim on our time than our family responsibilities? Where should our time go?

C. The family and the kingdom of God—dealing with the clash. All of us experience a clash between these two sets of responsibilities. The clash may be more acute at some times than at other times, but it is always there. Each individual has worked at the clash in one way or another. One thing that may be helpful is to let the group share moments in which these two sets of responsibilities have come into conflict and how the conflict was resolved.

As the group members share moments from their life stories, observe the different ways in which the conflict is resolved. Some people work on the basis of principle: e.g. on the principle that the family comes first. Another example of settling the responsibility clash on the basis of a principle was given by a physician. The physician defined his medical practice as his ministry. While discussing this case the physician offered: "The family knows that whenever there is a clash between the needs of my patients and the needs of the family, the needs of the patient have to come first. I do not like it that way any more than the family does, but that is the way it is. Sometimes I can turn the patient over to another physician, but that is not always possible. Either way the patient's needs come first."

Other people solve the clash on a "case by case" basis. One time they will decide to meet family needs and another time they will decide in favor of "ministerial" responsibilities. Why the family this time and the kingdom of God that time? Sometimes we try to operate by "keeping the score even." "The last time I decided for the family, so on this occasion my time will go into ministry." More often we try to go with the most "urgent" need. How do we decide the urgency of a need?

Finally it may be worthwhile for the discussion group to pursue changes that individuals or the group as a whole want to make in the future. As we look at our situation are we happy with the way we resolve the clash between family responsibility and our particular ministry as the body of Christ? What changes would you like to make in the future? Are there ways in which individuals or the group as a whole could assist you in making those changes? Does the group agree with the changes that you propose? Sometimes we misperceive what we need to do. We may think that we are neglecting the family or not doing enough in "ministry" while others read our situation much differently.

D. Putting the texts together. Look again at the two positions in the case. The first text states that one cannot use allegiance to the kingdom of God to avoid family responsibilities. The other argues that one cannot use family responsibilities to delay responding to one's "calling" as a Christian. The "Directions for Discussion" have implied that those two positions can stand without resolution. We can simply use them as poles within which to balance our lives. Do you agree? If not, how might you harmonize the clash between these two texts?

Even if we cannot harmonize them, perhaps we can explain them. How is it that we have two such disparate texts preserved in the Gospels? There are some suggestions in the "Concerns to Consider" and "Resources to Read" sections, but it might be enlightening to let the group explore this question before turning to answers provided by others.

E. Summary. The following steps are one way of exploring the issues in this case:
1. Where are we to give our time and energy?
   a. Our responsibilities as members of a family?
   b. Our responsibilities as members of the body of Christ?
2. What do we do when these responsibilities conflict?
3. How do we handle the clash between these two texts, both of which reflect values affirmed by Jesus?

Concerns to Consider
There are many issues that one might wish to explore in connection with this case. One might organize a discussion

around the question of "calling." What is a Christian "calling" which might cause a person to give that precedence over responsibility to family? How does a person know that he or she has such a "calling"? A related concern involves the kingdom of God. How can one identify the kingdom of God? How does an individual know that the work one understands to be a "calling" is actually related to the kingdom of God and not some other "kingdom"? It may be that the discussion leader will wish to orient the discussion around issues such as these rather than the one chosen under "Directions for Discussion." Or it may happen that these issues will be raised in the course of the case discussion. If so, the flow of the discussion period will be different from that proposed above.

(The plan suggested under "Directions for Discussion" concentrates on the factor of conflicting responsibilities. More particularly it is concerned with the conflicting responsibilities of family and the kingdom of God as this issue is presented in the biblical texts and as it presents itself to us in life.)

A. Defining the kingdom of God. First a word about the kingdom of God: It is much easier to identify precisely what we mean by family than it is to define what we mean by the kingdom of God. Nevertheless there are some things which can be said. First of all the kingdom of God cannot be automatically identified with the institutional church nor can it be identified completely separate from the church. Both of the extremes of viewpoint are common. Those who are within the church and find the church meaningful tend to identify churchwork with the work of God's kingdom. Both the history of biblical Israel and the words in Revelation addressed to seven churches in Asia Minor (1:9 *ff.*) warn against automatic identification. Nor is the reverse necessarily the case. Those who are angry with the church and observe the fallibility of the church and its people tend to identify the kingdom of God with the work of those saintly people who act like Christians ought to act, but who are in no way associated with a church. We need to take care not to dismiss the church just because the behavior of many people is not exemplary. Abraham, Jacob, David, and Peter are biblical examples that God can accomplish the work of the "kingdom" with people whose behavior is often problematic and whose allegiance to God is not always clear, even though they claim to be a part of God's people. How would you describe the relationship of the kingdom of God to the work of the church?

Second, the kingdom of God cannot be reduced to either a present reality or a future event. In the teachings of Jesus the kingdom of God is never equated with a present experience. There is a "not yet-ness" about the kingdom of God. On the other hand, one cannot say that the kingdom of God is only in the future. There is a "presentness" about the kingdom according to the New Testament. Where have you experienced the presence of the "kingdom"? In what way do you understand the kingdom of God as not yet here? Does "not yet" mean the "kingdom" is not yet complete for everybody, but that some people do experience the fullness of the "kingdom"? Or does it mean that everyone's experience of the "kingdom" is partial?

Finally, one cannot describe the kingdom of God. When Jesus was asked to describe the "kingdom," he told stories, parables. It is likely that we can do no better. We too can only tell stories about experiences, perhaps similar to those in the parables of Jesus. What parables come to mind as "kingdom" stories? Good Samaritan? Prodigal Son? What experience in your own pilgrimage would you describe as an experience of the kingdom of God, at least in a partial sense?

B. The kingdom versus the family. We are left then with no absolute definition of what the kingdom of God is to which the Christian is called to give allegiance. Be that as it may, Christians are responsible to identify the work of God's kingdom as best as their observation and study allow and undertake that work diligently. Having identified our work, there comes the inevitable clash between our responsibility to our family and to the kingdom of God.

Of course this clash is by no means unique to Christians. The physician mentioned above told about the clash between his work and his family responsibilities. He understood his work as the healing ministry of the kingdom of God, but many physicians do not. The class is the same. It is also the same for people in business and politics. Can you think of any person who has not had a conflict between one set of responsibilities and another?

There are many ways of resolving the clash between one's family and one's Christian responsibilities. Here is just a sampling. One might choose to give almost all of one's energy to one calling and let other people fulfill the other. An example of this is the Roman Catholic clergy and religious orders. In the Roman Catholic perspective some people are called to give full attention to the work of the "kingdom" while others are to care for families. There is a recognition that attempting to do both creates problems. In fairness one has to say that Roman Catholic tradition does not perceive either the calling to care for family or the calling to a "religious" vocation to be superior. They both have to be there. That is one way of resolving the tension between the texts. Is that an adequate resolution of the clash?

Protestants have most often said that the individual is called to do both, care for family and work in the "kingdom." Unpredictable things happen with that position, however. For example, spouses will sometimes have an uneven load of one or the other. In a clergy family, the person who is vocationally involved may carry the responsibility for the "kingdom" work while the other spouse (traditionally the wife) will care for the family. In a non-clergy family again one spouse may be more involved in one calling than the other. In this case it is often the wife who is actively working in the church or other kingdom-like services. The husband is too busy with job and family responsibilities. When he is not at "work," he is taking the kids fishing or camping, or he is resting so he can continue working to meet the family's physical needs. More and more this pattern is breaking down. Whom have you seen—either individuals or couples—who has been successful at working with a conflict of responsibilities? Where have you seen this clash not successfully resolved?

Finally there is another element that affects most of us. That is the matter of timing. We tend to resolve responsibility clashes in different ways at different times in our lives. Thomas Kelly in *A Testament of Devotion* acknowledges that there are times when one may not be able to engage in the disciplined devotions which he sees as the fundamental responsibility of every Christian. One of these times is when "the children are small." To be sure he is aware that we are inclined to put many things ahead of our Christian responsibility, which should *almost* never happen. But even he acknowledges that at *certain* times family responsibility can take precedence.

There may be times in our lives when family responsibilities should take precedence over all other work. There may be other times in our lives when we need to say "No" to a family responsibility in order to say "Yes" to another need. It may even be possible that there are stages in our lives when our family responsibilities must take precedence and other stages when we give most of our energy to responsibilities in our particular Christian "ministry." Many studies have been made on the matter of what activities are customary or appropriate for different moments in life's pilgrimage. One of the most popular is *Passages* by Gail Sheehy. She argues that there are times when we should give all our energy to realizing our own potential and other times for assisting others in realizing their potential. Both cannot be accomplished at the same time.

How does timing or one's stage in life enter into the question of family first or "kingdom" first? Is that an appropriate way to resolve the tension between the two?

C. Understanding the biblical text. As was stated above, it is very difficult to push these two texts so that they both say the same thing. Some people will want to find a unity which removes the difficulty, and it is helpful to listen to such attempts. Nevertheless, efforts to make these two texts completely harmonious are likely to be forced. Our inability to resolve the dichotomy in our own lives is mirrored in these two textual traditions. We cannot even handle the clash between the texts by saying that one comes from Jesus and the other does not. In the New Testament both are attributed to Jesus.

If we cannot resolve the difference so as to make both of them say the same thing, perhaps we can at least understand how such different texts both came to be attributed to Jesus. In the passages under discussion, it is not possible to establish precisely what Jesus said. The passage about the Corban in Mark 7:10-13 is a traditional anti–Pharisaic polemic. We cannot say that these are Jesus' words. In its present form these words probably come from the church. The clear element of continuity with Jesus is its insistence that no "churchly" ritual or responsibility should override fundamental human needs (see Mark 3:1-6).

Luke 14:26 and Matthew 10:37 also show continuity with Jesus' words. Similar sayings appear in Matthew 19:29 and Mark 10:29-30. But it is not possible to delineate which one or ones come from Jesus and which are applications of Jesus' words by the church. Clearly Jesus did affirm that the demands of the kingdom of God may supersede a person's responsibilities even in the most basic human relationships. On the other hand, the parables tend to show that the primary work of the "kingdom" is to meet human need wherever it may occur. Perhaps both sayings affirm human need to be the place where we give our time and energy. Neither family responsibilities nor anything else can be used as an "excuse." But of all the needs we see around us, to which do we respond first?

Resources to Read
Mark 7:9-13; Luke 14:25-33; Matthew 10:37-38

No religious practice in the name of obedience to God can justify neglecting one's responsibility to family. No family tie, however close, can be used as an excuse to delay or deny one's responsibility as a follower of Jesus.

Anderson, Hugh. *The Gospel of Mark* (New Century Bible Commentaries). Greenwood, South Carolina: Attic Press, 1976. Pp. 185-86.

The church valued this narrative in Mark 7:9-13 because it pictured Jesus as one who possessed an intuitive awareness of God's will. That awareness caused Jesus to put human needs and interests above everything else.

Caird, G. B. *The Gospel of St. Luke* (The Pelican Gospel Commentaries). New York: The Seabury Press, 1963. Pp. 178-79.

Ties to family must not be allowed to interfere with a person's absolute commitment to the kingdom of God. The family must take second place.

Perrin, Norman. *Jesus and the Language of the Kingdom.* Philadelphia: Fortress Press, 1976. Pp. 15-32, 40-56, 194-204.

The kingdom of God is a word symbol. It points beyond itself to a reality. The kingdom of God as used by Jesus is not a symbol that points only to one historical moment or event. It is a symbol that points to a given moment and later another moment and even a future moment. Jesus used "kingdom of God" in such a way that it cannot be limited to past, present, or future. It is an event which every person experiences in his or her own time, yesterday, today, and tomorrow.